Shawn Michaels is undoubtedly one of the greatest Superstars in WWE history and his story of redemption is an inspiration to us all. *Wrestling for My Life* takes readers on an incredible journey that ultimately illustrates the values I knew Shawn always possessed.

—*Vince McMahon*, WWE Chairman and CEO

Shawn's greatest challenge came from deep within himself, and it's been awe-inspiring to watch this man pull himself from the depths of his own personal hell by immersing himself in his faith in God. I couldn't be more amazed at the man, husband, father, and friend he has become.

—*The Undertaker*

I am certain that you will enjoy getting to know Shawn Michaels from the pages within as much as I have in his everyday life. If you read one book this year, make it this one!

—*Pastor Matthew Hagee*

Shawn's story is an important reminder of life's priorities and how we choose to use our given gifts. While I work with Shawn outside of the wrestling world, I can still strongly attest to his perseverance, passion, and humility. These pages offer an inside look into how he found strength for better change.

—*Jeff Wayne*, Executive Vice President Programming of Outdoor Channel

When Shawn started his second career in the hunting TV world, I was blessed to get to know Shawn Michaels, the man. His character, focus on God, and commitment to family and friends is inspiring.

—*Ronnie "Cuz" Strickland*, Vice President of Mossy Oak television and video productions

WRESTLING FOR MY

LIFE

WRESTLING FOR MY

LIFE

THE LEGEND, THE REALITY, AND THE FAITH OF A WWE SUPERSTAR

Shawn Michaels
with David Thomas

ZONDERVAN

Wrestling for My Life
Copyright © 2014 by Shawn Michaels

Requests for information should be addressed to:
Zondervan, 3900 *Sparks Drive SE, Grand Rapids, Michigan* 49546

This edition: 978-0-310-34754-5 (softcover)

Library of Congress Cataloging-in-Publication Data

Michaels, Shawn.
    Wrestling for my life / Shawn Michaels, with David Thomas. - 1st Edition.
        pages   cm
    Includes bibliographical references and index.
    ISBN 978-0-310-34078-2 (softcover : alk. paper)
    1. Michaels, Shawn. 2. Wrestlers - United States - Biography. I. Thomas,
David, 1970- II. Title.
    GV1196.M53A3   2015
    796.812092 - dc23 [B]   2014040222

Published in association with the agency of Encore Sports & Entertainment, LLC,
703 Palomar Airport Road, Suite 200, Carlsbad, CA 92011.

Cover photography and design: *Micah Kandros*
Interior illustration: *All photos were provided by the author unless otherwise noted.*
Interior design: *Kait Lamphere*

First Printing February 2016 / Printed in the United States of America

DEDICATION

When you get asked to do a dedication page, lots of things and people go through your head.

For me, first and foremost, my family: Rebecca, Cameron, and Cheyenne. My life! Plain and simple, without them I shudder to think where I would be. Mom, Dad, brothers, sister, friends—the list would go on.

For this book, I want to dedicate it to anyone and everyone who maybe is like me: Not totally sure of everything other than where they've been. And as they go forward, just want to do their best not to make the same mistakes, use the wisdom they've gained from those mistakes, and honor God the best way they know how. Now, I know that still allows a lot of room for error, but truthfully, I cling, in white-knuckle fashion, to the Scripture that "Man looks at the outside but God looks at the heart" because I know where my heart lies. And if you do too, but find yourself unsure (admittedly or not) about God's plan for you, His direction, or His will for your life and are just trying to do your best, then this book is for you.

"As for God, his way is perfect:
the word of the LORD is tried."
—PSALM 18:30 KJV

SPECIAL DEDICATION

Dad died [handwritten note in left margin]

My father passed away last summer as this book was being done. His tombstone reads: *Devoted Husband, Father, Patriot, He lived with honor.*

I mention that because, we, his family—sons, daughter, even Mom—may debate whether Dad was good at this or that, but no one has ever questioned my father's devotion or his honor. Everyone who ever met him has said the same thing.

I've thought a lot about that since my father's passing. What will they say about me? Now hear me clearly on this: I didn't say what will "people" say; I said what will "they"—my family—say about me? And the reason I emphasize this, though it may be harsh, is that "people" weren't by my father's side when he passed, nor will they be by mine. It will be family.

w/Dad [handwritten note in left margin]
I died [handwritten note in left margin]
My father was the first person I've ever watched die … I was right by his side, my hand on his heart as he breathed his last breath here and his first breath in eternity.

All I could think about was what a great man he was and how fortunate I was to get to be there by his side.

I say all this to emphasize: what will your family say about you? That's what it all comes down to. Respectfully, friends, business associates, fans, you name it—they likely won't be there. We get caught up in so much that is trivial and unfortunately forsake so much that isn't. My tombstone won't say "I lived with honor," because for much of my life, before I found Christ, I didn't do so. But I'm still here … and so are you! This world doesn't let us forget our past, but the Creator of the universe does! Don't let anyone tell you what your tombstone will say. Begin today, like my father, to be devoted to those who love you and to live with honor.

CONTENTS

FOREWORD

PAUL "TRIPLE H" LEVESQUE

I was sitting on the bed in my hotel room getting ready for a show in Birmingham, Alabama, when I got the call from Kevin Nash asking if I would speak to Shawn Michaels. I didn't know how I felt about it.... Of course I would talk to him, but Shawn and I hadn't spoken in a long time.

For six years we had been best friends, almost like family. We were together more than we were apart, riding up and down the road more than 300 days a year. There is nothing we wouldn't do for each other. But ultimately, Shawn's addictions and self-destruction had pushed me away.

"Hunter, it's Shawn." It was so good to hear his voice, because it sounded different. He wasn't slurring his words. He didn't sound bitter and angry, like the Shawn who would say things he knew would hurt you the worst, just to make you feel as bad as he did. There was a clarity and a sincerity to his voice ... and I hadn't heard that Shawn in a very long time.

He asked me for my forgiveness. I was blown away. "Forgiveness" struck me, because it wasn't something the Shawn I knew would say. In the past, Shawn was always defensive, almost unapologetic for his actions. I wasn't sure if I should believe Shawn at first, but I was elated at the thought of having my best friend back. Even more than that, I was relieved to unload the burden that on any given day, Shawn might die. He had found the path back to his life, and I couldn't be happier.

Shawn called HHH asked to comeback [handwritten]

Then he hit me with another request. After four years of retirement, Shawn asked if he could come back to WWE for one more match, and he said he wanted that match to be with me. Shawn said he wanted his son to watch him wrestle, but I knew the reason ran much deeper than that. Shawn wanted to go out on his terms; he wanted to end his career his way, with one more moment in the spotlight. This match represented closure. The "Heartbreak Kid," Shawn Michaels, is one of the greatest performers in the history of our industry, and I was honored he wanted to dance his last dance with me.

At SummerSlam 2002, one of WWE's biggest pay-per-view events, I wrestled Shawn in front of a sold-out crowd in the Nassau Military Veterans Coliseum in Uniondale, New York, not knowing whether or not he could still physically perform. Truthfully, I don't know if Shawn knew for sure either. Thirty seconds in, I knew Shawn was still the best I had ever stepped in the ring with. For forty minutes we blew the roof off the building and had what for me, for many reasons, would be one of my most memorable matches. In my mind, that match closed the door on the past and opened the door to Shawn reviving his career and getting his life on track. Most importantly to me, I had my "brother" back.

most memorable matches [handwritten margin note]

I watched Shawn continue down his path and ultimately become the best husband, best father, and quite possibly the best man I know. This book will take you on Shawn's journey and show you how his faith helped him find himself again.

Hunter + Shawn together again [handwritten margin note]

Shawn, I love you, my brother.

—Hunter

Before you turn another page, you need to ask
yourself one question, "Are You Ready?"

FOREWORD

"STONE COLD" STEVE AUSTIN

It's always nice to see Shawn Michaels these days. We both proudly come from the same line of work, professional wrestling. The pro wrestling scene back in the day was like the Wild Wild West. We traveled all over the world wrestling and living like rock stars. Shawn Michaels was one of the greatest performers in the history of the business.

Shawn and I rarely crossed paths back in our early days. But finally I made it to the big leagues, WWE, where Shawn was one of the top guys in the territory. Every night I saw Shawn light up a crowd like only he could. Inside the ring Shawn was a king. Outside the ring he was cocky, arrogant, and self-centered. We wrestled on many occasions. Business was business. But outside the ring we never talked. Other than work, we had nothing in common, and quite frankly, on a personal level, I did not care for him, his attitude, or his antics.

I won my first World Championship from Shawn at *Wrestle-Mania 14* in Boston, Massachusetts. No one in the WWE was even sure Shawn was going to go in the ring that night, including myself. After that night, I went my way, and Shawn went his. Somewhere along the way, Shawn found God. I can't remember how, so I'll let him tell that story. I will tell you this:

The Shawn Michaels you see today is a stand-up guy. He is a man's man. He is a straight shooter. If he looks you in the eye and gives you his word, consider it done. Shawn has always had a great

[handwritten margin note: Didn't like Shawn]

sense of humor, and these days I can laugh along and joke with him because he has left all of his insecurities and arrogance behind. Confidence, peace, and a self-deprecating sense of humor are what I now see in Shawn. I saw glimpses of this back in the day, but now it is truly who he is.

Nowadays, Shawn and I have come full circle. I'll go on the record as admitting I have made a few self-improvements as well. We have many things in common now. Family comes first and foremost. A love of the great outdoors, hunting, camping, a close circle of friends, and a four-wheel drive truck are the first things that come to mind.

They say the Lord works in mysterious ways, and I guess they are right. Because he surely worked a miracle with a man that I am now proud to call my friend.

INTRODUCTION

As a twelve-year-old growing up in San Antonio, Texas, I dreamed of wrestling for a living. That was all I wanted to do, and when I allowed my imagination to run free, I could envision myself lifting Southwest Championship Wrestling's heavyweight championship belt high above my head.

That was it. That was the best I could see my life becoming. That was the most I felt I could even dream of accomplishing.

Fortunately, there were people in my life who saw even more in me. I don't know, perhaps they saw me winning some of the string of championships I eventually achieved in the sport. But I doubt that any of them—especially the ones in those earliest years—could look down the road and see my name on the list included in debates over who is the greatest professional wrestler of all time.

I now know something that none of us knew at the time: I had been placed on a path that would lead me to the top of our sport, and those who would help me reach the pinnacle had been positioned alongside that path.

My objective back then was to wrestle. Nothing more than that. But all along, I would come to learn, God held a greater purpose for my life.

That is what has led me to write this book.

I can assure you that the Texas teen who needed to be put into a submission hold in order to read a book could not have imagined that eventually he would write a book, much less two books.

Almost a decade has passed since the release of my first book, *Heartbreak & Triumph: The Shawn Michaels Story,* thanks to the work of co-writer Aaron Feigenbaum. I enjoyed sharing the story of my life and career, but that was a book for wrestling fans that World Wrestling Entertainment (WWE) had asked me to produce. I had been a Christian for about two years when we wrote that book, and while I was free to share how I had come to accept Jesus Christ as my Lord and Savior and about the early days of my Christian walk, we didn't go into much detail about my spirituality because we were writing primarily a wrestling book.

This second book, however, is one I have desired to write. I know the attraction for many readers will be their curiosity about my return to wrestling, the circumstances surrounding my second retirement, and my life since, including my venture into outdoors television. And while I won't gloss over any of those ventures, my career will not be the ultimate story here as it was in my first book. Instead, I want to write a book that focuses more on the spiritual side of my life.

I don't think the best way to describe this book is "writing my life story for a second time." I prefer to view this one as telling the story of my second life—the one God has given me, and the one that has ignited me with new purpose.

Faith has transformed my life. Ask the guys who knew me in the wrestling business before my salvation, and they will tell you it has been a complete change—and a needed change. I know, because many have told me both.

Wrestling used to be my entire identity. Before becoming a Christian, I was known by such nicknames as The Heartbreak Kid, The Showstopper, The Headliner, The Main Event. Looking back, it is fitting that all those were derived exclusively from what I accomplished in the ring. In earning those names, I had been a wrestler and nothing more.

When I exited the ring for the final time, I walked away with complete peace. That would not have happened without my faith. If I had not been a Christian when I retired, I probably would have been another one of those athletes who struggled miserably through the transition to life after competition. But when I left, being a wrestler

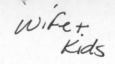

was no longer my identity. Being a good husband to my wife, Rebecca, and a good father to my two children, Cameron and Cheyenne, had already become far more important than any title I could earn in the ring.

I said in my farewell speech that I was leaving to spend more time with my family, and I meant it. I have stayed true to my word.

While I recognized that I had made an impact on wrestling, there was a place to which God had called me to make a more significant impact: my home. I had made my name in the ring, but at home was where I desired to build my legacy.

I even view my career differently since writing the first book. Wrestling was such a busy job then that there was little time to pause and reflect on what was happening to me and around me. I have had time to do that now. Plus, my continued growth as a Christian offers a different perspective on my career. I took too many things for granted when I was wrestling, but now I continue to offer thanks for my career.

I wrestled for the last time in March 2010. I lost that match. Still, I left the ring a winner partly because God had given me a long and wonderful career in wrestling, but more so because He had given me something greater than I could have ever dreamed for myself.

A new life.

CHAPTER 1
FEELING AT HOME

"Great peace have those who love your law, and nothing can make them stumble" (Psalm 119:165).

Tears filled my eyes as I sat on the end of the bed.

The scene was familiar, but the feelings weren't. Another *Wrestle-Mania* had been completed and, as usual, I had returned to the hotel with my family and taken a couple of minutes to sit alone and reflect on the night before joining the family for a post-match celebration.

But this time was different. This was the last time. Overwhelmed with gratitude for the career now suddenly behind me, I could not help but notice the symbolism of what I was about to do next: get up from where I was sitting and walk away to join my family.

Sure, I'm a wrestler, yet in a business where "never" never means "never" when there's a good storyline to sell, I knew I would never wrestle again. Only a few hours before, I had lost to The Undertaker (Mark Calaway) at *WrestleMania 26* in a match with the stipulation that if I lost, I must retire. But, hey, if it would have made for a big-bucks pay-per-view for WWE, we could have found a way for me to un-retire. There also could have been a Shawn Michaels Farewell Tour, and we had discussed one.

But *I* knew this was the end. I had stepped out of the ring for the last time to step into the life I wanted to live: with my family, back home in Texas.

First Retirement 1998

I had retired once before, twelve years earlier, in 1998. That time, though, wasn't on the terms I wanted. I was forced to retire. After fourteen years of being subjected to a merciless pounding that I chose to inflict on myself, my body kicked me out of the ring. I hadn't liked how my final match had turned out, either. I had agreed to go out with a loss to "Stone Cold" Steve Austin, but had rejected WWE's idea for how they wanted to send me out of the ring the final time. It happened anyway. That had angered me because it hadn't provided me the respect I thought I deserved after all I had done for WWE.

lost to Stone Cold

no respect

Worse, my life was a wreck. Only in the ring could I be what I wanted to be. And that wasn't the real me. That was a wrestling character created and altered when needed to put on a good show. And that's what I did.

Somehow, I had found this ability to make fans react. Some loved me. Some hated me. But none, it seemed, didn't experience some kind of strong reaction when hearing before a match, "Making his way to the ring ... from San Antonio, Texas ... The Heartbreak Kid ... Shawn ... Michaels!"

I liked being loved. And I liked being hated. I might even have liked being hated more. But outside of that ring, my life had spiraled so out of control—drinking too much, chasing women, doing drugs, popping pills—that I did not like who I really was. A winner in the business, I had become a loser in life.

Then twelve years later, everything had changed.

Oh, my body still hurt. Still does, even five years after I packed up my wrestling gear for the final time and tossed the bag into the attic. Injuries were not the reason I was leaving this time, however. I retired because of my wife and kids, who had come to Arizona with me to watch my final match.

failing

I had discovered a new life since my first retirement. I was close to failing as a husband and on my way to failing as a father when I found that new life. I never would have imagined that I could feel so at peace with leaving wrestling. I certainly hadn't felt this way the first time I retired.

18

That is why I felt engulfed by peace as I sat alone on the end of the bed, appreciative for the wrestling career I had been given and grateful for the second chance I had received as a husband and father.

"Thank You, Lord," I prayed through my tears. *2nd retirement*

———————————

The thought that it was time to leave the ring for good first came a year earlier, after *WrestleMania 25* in 2009. In the first of three main events at Houston's Reliant Stadium, I took on The Undertaker. From a pure wrestling standpoint, it was an intriguing matchup: me—Mr. WrestleMania—against the wrestler with a 16–0 record in *WrestleManias*.

When we met to start setting up how the match would play out *Last Match vs Taker* three days before *WrestleMania*, Pat Patterson and Michael Hayes— who produced matches for WWE—told us we would not be one of the last two matches on the schedule and would wrestle for fifteen minutes.

"How long you been with this company?" Taker asked me.

"Lord knows how long, but it's been a while," I told him with a laugh.

"I've been with this company longer than some of my marriages combined!" Taker said.

Not being the main event or semi-main event motivated Taker and me to put on a match that would be a tough act to follow for the rest of the night. (We also wound up wrestling for thirty minutes, well past our allotted time.)

To add to the anticipation of the match, because I had been a Christian for seven years at that point and had made sure the changes in my life were evident inside the ring and out, we employed a light versus darkness theme. I entered the ring first, wearing white and *26* descending to a brightly lit stadium floor via a platform enveloped in white smoke. Then The Undertaker, dressed in his customary black, rose from below the stage floor and, in a darkened stadium, defiantly strolled toward the ring to his ominous theme music. WWE puts on good productions, and that one was really cool.

Taker and I turned in what I still consider a near-perfect match,

Perfect match

Taker dives on cameraman

despite one scare. About fifteen minutes into the match, we had planned for Taker to do a "dive." I would be lying outside of the ring, "hurt," and referee Marty Elias—a good friend whom I prayed with before every match we did together—would be checking on me to see if I would be able to return to the ring and continue the match. After I made my way to my feet, Taker would run across the ring and dive at me headfirst over the top rope. But I would see Taker coming, shove Marty out of the way, and pull a "cameraman" into my place. The cameraman would appear to take the hit instead of me, reaching out to catch Taker in the process and breaking Taker's fall.

Of course, with our old-school mentality, we weren't about to practice Taker's dive, or anything else for that matter. Nowadays it's different, but our mindset back then was that if we were going to miss a move or if anything would go wrong, it would happen during the pay-per-view when it was for real. When it came time for Taker's dive, the "cameraman" set up a step too far from the ring. I shoved Marty aside as planned, grabbed the cameraman, and tried to pull him closer to where Taker would land. But I couldn't get him to where I wanted. He dropped his camera and reached out toward Taker, but barely got his hands on Taker, who hit the padded floor headfirst.

When we had set up the match, both of us had instructed Marty that if for any reason neither of us was able to make it back into the ring after the dive, Marty was to go ahead and proceed with the referee's ten count as usual. If Taker or I couldn't make it back into the ring before the ten count, the match would be over right there. So after Marty and I returned to the ring, the referee started his ten count— but slowly and dramatically to play it up—while Taker remained flat on his back on the floor. I didn't know if Taker would get up. I was on the far side of the ring and didn't have a real good view of where he was, but Taker managed to crawl under the bottom rope and back into the ring right before Marty reached ten.

Taker was hurt, but we were able to finish out the match as planned. About fifteen minutes after the failed dive, the planned finish came when I performed my moonsault—a backflip off the top

almost a
perfect
Match

rope—and Taker caught me and dropped me with his Tombstone Piledriver for the pin.

A perfect match isn't possible, but that one came close. At one point, the more than 70,000 fans had started chanting, "This is awesome! This is awesome!" I already sensed inside the ropes that we were putting on a good show, and the fans' spontaneous chants confirmed my feelings.

Marty and I left the ring before Taker. When we walked through the curtain into the backstage area, the other wrestlers and crew members were standing and applauding. When Taker came through the curtain, he hobbled directly into the trainer's room and fell to the floor. I went in there with Marty while the trainers looked at Taker. Other wrestlers started coming in and out, checking on Taker and raving about our match.

"How am I going to go out and top that match?" asked Triple H, my best friend, who would be wrestling in the final match of the night.

WM
26

Michael Hayes came into the room. "Oh my!" he exclaimed. "What did I just witness?"

The answer, as wrestling fans still say, was one of the best matches in the history of professional wrestling.

Great
Match

Because that *WrestleMania* was in Houston, I was able to ride back home to San Antonio with my family the next day. Usually after a *WrestleMania*, it was off to the airport for the next night's *Raw* live television broadcast. "*WrestleMania* was great," Vince liked to tell us, "but that was yesterday and we have *Raw* tonight." Even after our biggest event of the year, it was right back to work to start building toward the next year's biggest event.

But that year, I had arranged to take a few months off following *WrestleMania*. At age forty-four, I wasn't wrestling full-time anyway. With a nine-year-old son and a daughter nearing five, I already was cutting back on my time away from home, and I was taking a break to think about how much longer I wanted to wrestle.

retired
at 44

WM
Thoughts

Rebecca and I had discussed how soon I would quit the sport, and that day, while she was driving the four of us home, I still managed to surprise her.

"You know," I told her, "that may have been the one to end it on."

"Really?" she asked.

"Yeah! I just don't know if it can get any better than that."

"Well," she told me, "that is a decision you're going to have to make pretty quick."

"I know," I answered. "We'll see."

I felt the satisfaction of a job well done after a great many of my matches. After the Taker match in Houston, though, I felt something different: a complete peace.

In some respects, wrestling can be like a drug addiction. Putting on a good match gives you a high, and you keep chasing that high. Or as my good friend Mark Calaway likes to say, "chasing the dragon." But I think for the first time, in the break I took after *WrestleMania 26*, I realized that I no longer was pursuing that high.

The contentment, the peace, and the completion that remained with me after we returned home were unlike anything I had felt in the business. *A Peace & Retire*

As I contemplated the possibility of never gearing up for another match, I was fine with it. And although it had been my public identity since I was nineteen, even the idea of not being identified as *Shawn Michaels the wrestler* didn't bother me.

Being okay with not feeling that high in the ring anymore, with not being *that* Shawn Michaels anymore, signaled to me that I was ready to retire. My four months off gave me the opportunity to practice being retired, if you will, and none of my feelings changed during that period.

Confirmation came when the time neared for me to return to WWE. Michael Hayes, the former wrestler who helped produce matches, called with an angle for the next *WrestleMania*. (An "angle" in wrestling is essentially a storyline or gimmick.)

"We have never done this before, but what do you think about this?" Michael began. "That match that you had with The Undertaker was amazing. I don't know how we can top it, but what if we do a rematch, and we put your career on the line?"

He even brought up the idea that it wouldn't be a true retirement, that we could bill the match as I would have to retire if I lost, yet come up with some creative way of getting around it if that's the route we wanted to take.

I told Michael I would think about it.

There was a lot to consider.

The Taker match would be a difficult one to follow, but the jock in me responded positively, not only to the possibility of that challenge, but also to being part of a storyline that WWE had not done. Having my career on the line would move what I had been thinking about, praying about, and believing that I was ready to do into a place where, publicly, there would be no turning back in my mind. If we were to say I would leave if I lost, I would leave if I lost.

I came back for the *SummerSlam* pay-per-view in August for a partial, mini-reunion of D-Generation X with Hunter (Paul Levesque). Hunter (also known as Triple H) and I, along with "Ravishing" Rick Rude and our female bodyguard, Chyna, had formed DX, as we were called for short, in the late 1990s. We and "Stone Cold" were the ones who had ushered in and then fueled the "Attitude Era" of what then was still known as the World Wrestling Federation. That was in my pre-Christian days, and we embraced the role of being the bad boys and girl of WWF.

Our characters were crude and broke all the rules. We didn't care whom we offended. I doubt wrestling has ever had a more controversial group than DX.

Hunter and I had reunited as a two-man DX for a short while in 2006, and we did so again when I came back from my time off after *WrestleMania 25*. Our storyline then was that after losing to Taker, I had become chef at an office cafeteria in Texas and Triple H came down to convince me to return and reform DX with him.

In December 2010, on a *Raw* episode taped in Corpus Christi,

Texas, I was to receive the WWE's Slammy Award—think Oscar or Grammy for wrestling—for Match of the Year from the *WrestleMania* match with The Undertaker. As Vince can attest, it's never too early to promote *WrestleMania*, and with the next one four months away, I started asking around to find out if we were going to go through with the rematch idea at *WrestleMania 26*. I was told a decision had not been made.

On the night I was to receive the Slammy, just a few minutes before I was to go out into the arena, I followed up with Vince and Michael to find out whether we had an answer yet on the rematch.

"Why?" I was asked.

"Because if we are," I replied, "why don't I go out there and accept this award from that match and then say to Taker, 'Match of the Year is not good enough. I do that all the time. I know I can beat you,' and then lay out a challenge to him."

That sparked a hurried discussion, but the consensus seemed to be that we shouldn't rush into a decision.

Before I became a Christian, I had been difficult to work with, making demands based on how I thought storylines should go and such. I had strong opinions on how we should do things and was no-holds-barred on expressing them. I was the source of a lot of Vince's stress. Jim Ross, the WWE announcer, used to tell me, "It wasn't what you were saying, it was your presentation." Jim was spot on.

So I had a reputation for holding the decision-makers' feet to the fire. I was still going to do that as a Christian, but in a much more respectful and unselfish way.

"Come on," I told them. "What else am I going to say out there? What am I going to do?"

"I don't know," Vince said. "What are you thinking?"

"Well, if I go out there and say it, we have to do it, right?"

"Geez," Vince said, "don't do that."

"Well, we need to make a decision," I announced. "Either we are going to do this thing or we aren't."

"I think we ought to do it," Michael said.

"What about the career and everything else?" Vince asked. "What are we going to do there?"

"I don't know," I said. "I have some ideas."

Having some ideas didn't seem to convince them of anything.

"I don't know," Vince said. "It's your call. I'm just not sure if we go there."

By this point, the announcement for the award was being made.

"We are going there," I said.

"Are you going to do it?" Michael asked.

"I think I am. I will just lay the challenge out there, and we'll see what happens."

"I guess we're going there then," Vince said.

I went out and, after making my acceptance speech, stepped away from the microphone, then went back and issued the challenge for a rematch.

The fans in Corpus Christi ate it up.

Mark Calaway was sitting at home, watching on television. *Retire*

"What?!" Mark asked his television. *after WM 26*

Like many events in my career, the decision to set the retirement plan in motion came down to a feeling. *26*

In the lead-up to *WrestleMania 26*, we brought in the retirement *2010* aspect. The discussions continued to include the possibility that it *?* would not be a true career-ender for me, suggesting I could take a year off and then make another comeback. After all, I had taken four months off after the last *WrestleMania*, so they figured I could be *Live* happy with an entire year off and still be available for them to use *T.V.* here and there on a part-time basis. They seemed to prefer a farewell *USA* tour over an abrupt retirement. Michael Hayes knew I was seriously considering walking away, although I don't think anyone in WWE knew how much I was looking forward to a permanent retirement.

But I knew that would be my last match. My career was ending.

My match with The Undertaker was the final match of *Wrestle-Mania 26*. With Taker putting his unbeaten *WrestleMania* streak on the line and my retirement at stake, the match was billed as "Streak vs. Career."

We didn't top the previous year's match—I still don't think we could have—but as far as sequels go, we put on a very good show.

When I was being trained to try to make it in the sport, long-time wrestler Jose Lothario had convinced me to learn how to do a backflip off the top rope. Jose had seen only one wrestler master that move. When an opponent was running toward me in the corner, I could scale the turnbuckles and backflip over my opponent and land on my feet so that when the opponent turned around to look for me, I could surprise him with an elbow or bust his chops some other way.

The backflip helped me quickly rise with the reputation as an athletic wrestler in the early stages of my career. It also led to my later developing my "moonsault," a different type of jump, in which I would flip backward off the top rope and, instead of landing on my feet, come down headfirst and stomach to shoulders with my opponent so he could catch me or break my fall to help me slide into finishing the move.

The night before *WrestleMania*, Rebecca and I were at University of Phoenix Stadium going over the match with Mark and Michael. There was an announcer's table outside the ring, and I brought up the idea of The Undertaker lying on that table and me moonsaulting onto him and both of us crashing through the table. I had never attempted the move like that.

I looked to the table. It was probably twelve feet from the ring.

Geez, I thought, *that's a long way.*

I climbed up on the top rope to get a better idea of what the flip would look like.

"That's a long way," Michael said. Then he looked to Rebecca and asked what she was thinking.

Rebecca looked at me on the top rope, looked to Mark, and looked back at me.

"He'll make it," she said.

During the match, when I moonsaulted out of the ring and onto

Moonsault

Taker on the table, the crowd went absolutely nuts. I loved it that in my very last match I was able to pull off something I had never attempted. Taker won the match when he pinned me after a third Tombstone Piledriver. (I had kicked out after the first two.) As good as the match was, to me the best part came in the ring afterward.

I need to back up here to my first retirement, back in 1998. I had been wrestling for several years with a hurt back among other injuries, but I really messed it up further in a match against The Undertaker, of all people, when I got tossed over the top rope and out of the ring and then hit my back on, of all things, a casket sitting ringside as a prop.

A few days later at home, I woke up with my back in such pain that I had to be taken to the hospital by ambulance. An MRI revealed that I had two herniated discs and one crushed disc.

Vince had me visit a doctor in New York, who told me that I would never wrestle again. I wanted to wrestle in *WrestleMania 14*, and I returned home to San Antonio to be treated by my doctor, who affirmed that the risk was too great for me to get back into the ring even one more time. I was supposed to drop the WWF Championship to Steve Austin in the main event, so I told my doctor I had to wrestle and I needed him to help make it happen.

I underwent two months of therapy to get my back as ready as it could be for the final match. I wasn't in good shape when I went to *WrestleMania*, but I was good enough to put on one more show. Steve asked me before the match what we needed to do to make sure I made it through, and he set up a match my back could handle.

Mike Tyson, who was then on a forced leave from boxing after he had bitten off part of Evander Holyfield's ear during a fight, was brought in to serve as a special ring-side enforcer. The match was set up so that the referee would get knocked out, Steve would drop me with his Stone Cold Stunner, and then Tyson would take the referee's place and count me out. Afterward, I would get up and begin protesting to Tyson, who would land a knockout punch to my jaw.

I was good with everything until Pat Peterson stepped in and said that Tyson should follow his knockout punch by draping one of

Steve's "Austin 3:16" T-shirts over me. That was too much for me. I felt I was really taking one for the team by wrestling when I shouldn't be, and I was fine with the match setup and dropping the belt to Steve. But I thought the shirt bit was insulting to my career, and I threatened to walk out until Pat relented and agreed to drop the shirt from the plan.

My back was killing me, and I struggled to do anything well in the ring, but Steve got me through the match and everything went as planned up through the Tyson punch. However, while I was KOed on the mat, Tyson laid an Austin 3:16 shirt over me. That wasn't supposed to happen!

Now I can look back and see how Pat wasn't being mean-spirited. He was simply looking to end the show by crowning Steve as the new guy for a new era of WWE. It was the right move for WWE to do, but I was too angry and bitter back then to want that to happen. I was only concerned about me. I felt insulted, and I made a bigger deal out of it than I should have—trying to save some face, I guess.

With Hunter alongside me, I stormed toward the post-match news conference of Steve and Tyson. I intended to kick open the door to interrupt and raise a big stink in front of the media, but Shane McMahon, Vince's son, met me at the door and calmed me down to the point that, although I was still upset, I at least walked away.

It was bad enough that doctors were the ones telling me I had to stop wrestling, but then the big switch pulled off on me really made me feel as if I was being forced out by more than my physical problems.

The aftermath of The Undertaker match, however, was a perfect way for me to go into retirement for good. Following the Tombstone Piledriver, I remained "out" on the mat for probably three minutes while Taker gradually made his way to his feet and gathered enough strength to walk around the ring again. Then Taker came over to me, helped me to my feet, and leaned me against the ropes.

Mark then said something to me that I have never disclosed publicly although I have been asked many times. Wrestling is a make-believe business, but there are times when we wrestlers get to have real moments inside the ring. We often keep those to ourselves, partly because wrestling's loyal fans can have a difficult time separating what is real from what isn't. But more so because those moments—and they are infrequent moments—create a special bond between guys who often spend more time with each other than with their families and, literally, trust each other with their lives inside the ring. So I have chosen to keep that quick exchange private.

Taker reached out his hand to shake mine. We embraced as the fans roared, then Taker left the ring to leave me there alone to accept the cheers of the 70,000-plus fans. I blew a kiss to the fans, waved, and dropped to my knees and raised my hands toward heaven.

I appreciated Mark and everyone involved at WWE for allowing me that moment, especially in light of what had taken place with my first retirement.

A little later in a private room inside the stadium, still sweaty and in my wrestling gear, I was sitting at a table with Mark and Michael. The three of us had had the same meeting a year earlier after my first *WrestleMania* match with The Undertaker.

Small smiles were on all three of our faces as we soaked in what had taken place in the ring, discussing how the ending could not have gone better. I still look back fondly on that conversation, because it was special for Mark and me to be able to share that final match. Also, Michael loved being a part of it due to all the contributions he had made to WWE.

For the first time it started to settle into my mind that, *Wow, that really was the last one!* I was done with chasing the dragon.

Michael's smile gave way to an all-business look.

"Let me ask you something," he said to me.

"Okay."

"What do you think about that retirement tour?"

I leaned back in my chair, soaking in the question for just an extra second before saying, "I'm not feeling it."

I paused before explaining, "How do you come back after that? I just don't see it. I'm done."

Michael processed my answer, then responded, "I'm not feeling it, either."

Farewell Raw speech on the next night

_____

That *was* the end. They knew it, and I knew it. And never in wrestling had I experienced such a deep-reaching peace.

The following night on *Raw*, I was given the opportunity to make a farewell address to the fans.

"Take as long as you want," I was told. Fortunately for the producers, I'm not one for long goodbyes.

Before I started speaking from the center of the ring, the bell gonged from the opening of The Undertaker's theme song. Mark stepped out onto the stage, tipped his black hat to me, then turned and walked back into the darkness.

speech

As I began to speak, the fans started chanting, "Please don't go! Please don't go!" Nice touch, but they were not talking me out of this decision.

I thanked the fans and told them they probably were unaware that there was a time when all I had in my life were the fans and how the ring was the only place where I felt good about myself. I was afraid to start thanking people because I knew I would leave out someone important, but there were a few names I had to mention. Feeling tears in my eyes, I thanked Hunter for being a friend when others in the business didn't want to be my friend—and rightfully so because of my attitude, I added. I thanked the production people behind the scenes at WWE; my one-time rival, Bret Hart; and Vince McMahon.

As I began to conclude, I thanked my Lord and Savior, Jesus Christ. "I thank you, my King, for saving me."

My last round of thanks went to Rebecca, Cheyenne, and Cameron.

"Babies," I told them, "Daddy's coming home."

CHAPTER 2
FROM BOTTOM UP

*"Very truly I tell you, no one can see the kingdom of
God unless they are born again" (John 3:3).*

The rock-bottom moment in my life began on the living room couch.

Cameron was barely two, and it was our weekly pizza-and-cookies night. Every Friday, we would pig out on pizza—pepperoni and jalapeno for me, cheese for him—and chocolate chip cookies. Cameron loved our Friday nights. I did too.

But on this Friday night, I was in another one of my pill-induced fogs, stretched out on the couch, only half aware of what was going on around me. In the middle of eating cookies, Cameron crawled up on me, pretended to be asleep, and then said, "Daddy's tired."

I hear his words today more crisply than I did that night, because that was the moment I can look back to and realize that, unbeknownst to me, Cameron had figured out what I was.

It was close to Cameron's bedtime, and Rebecca offered to take him to his room and read him a bedtime story.

"No, I'll do it," I adamantly countered.

I read to my son almost every night because I so wanted to be a good dad. Even if I wasn't one.

I followed Cameron off to his bedroom and read to him. There's

Becoming he
aware was drugged
at

no chance of my remembering the name of the book because, in the state I was in, it was all I could do to slur my way through the story. When I finished reading, I went back to the couch and fell asleep.

Rebecca later helped me to bed, and during the night I woke up and shook her.

"Who ate the cookies?" I asked, unable to recall what had happened during the night.

"You did," she answered.

I couldn't remember eating the pizza and cookies, but that was the answer I expected.

Angry at myself, I stormed to the bathroom and flipped on the light.

"I ate them?" I asked Rebecca again.

"Yeah, you ate them," she repeated.

Sobbing almost uncontrollably, I stared at the man in the mirror directly into his eyes and told him that he was a piece of trash.

God

Disgusted with what I was seeing—*who* I was seeing—I returned to bed. For the first time, reality had set in: My son was beginning to notice who I truly was, and that was going to affect him. I was in the process of ruining not only my life, but also my son's.

"Lord," I said. "Please change me."

The Lord and I didn't exactly have a history of open communication. In fact, I think that night was the first time I ever cried out to Him. I had grown up attending church and knew who God is, but I didn't know *Him*. I did, however, know enough about God to recognize that I was not living the way I was supposed to be living.

Nash
Phone call

The next day, Kevin Nash called me.

Kevin and I had been close friends since 1993, when he left World Championship Wrestling to join WWE as my bodyguard and best friend.

We had talked the night before, and he called me again because he was concerned about how I had sounded. He asked if I was still doing pills. "Every once in a while," I answered.

Kevin
Nash
aware

At one point, I had been popping thirty to thirty-five pills a day,

36

Somas *downers—* *Pain Killers*

mostly muscle relaxers, to help deal with the pain resulting from more than fifteen years of wrestling. I had cut back to only on the weekends and, by comparison, that did seem like "every once in a while" to me. I had convinced myself that not taking pills every day was a major accomplishment.

But Kevin read me the riot act over the phone. To him, even *Riot act* every once in a while was way too often if it happened in front of my *Kevin Nash* family.

"Dude, you have a wife and a son. You can't be doing this anymore."

The conversation with Kevin replayed in my mind throughout the day. The next morning, I rolled over in bed and told Rebecca that I was done with the drugs for good.

"That's great," she replied, though sounding unconvinced.

She had heard me say that before.

The first time I had sworn off drugs and alcohol was when we had learned that Rebecca was pregnant with Cameron.

You're going to be having a child, I told myself. *You have to get your-* *Broken Promise* *self together.*

I didn't.

When I look back, I honestly don't believe or know that I was an addict. I say that because I think I could have stopped popping the pills and getting drunk. It was just that I didn't want to. So after vowing to stop, I granted myself a waiver. It wasn't really necessary to stop at that point, I convinced myself, when I could wait until our child actually arrived.

Of course, when Cameron was born, I didn't stop.

He's just a baby, I reasoned. *He isn't old enough to know what you're doing.*

In my mind, though, desperate to acknowledge anything good *Drugs only* about myself, I thought it was commendable that I had reduced my *on weekends* drug use to only on weekends.

But I was still doing them. And that night after what happened on the couch, I realized that for almost three years I had kept fooling

33

"Daddy's Tired"

myself to the point that my son had become old enough to know that there were times when Daddy would be "tired."

The notion that at least cutting back on my drug use made me worthy of a pat on my back was a direct product of how I had grown up.

I was a pretty good kid who didn't get into a lot of trouble. I listened to my parents, although since I was the son of an Air Force officer, there were times when it seemed I didn't have any options other than to do as told. We were widely regarded as a good family.

I was the last of four children, with two brothers and a sister. My second-to-oldest brother and my sister found a little bit of trouble growing up, but my oldest brother and I avoided serious trouble. Our brother and sister were the ones who established the negative bar, so to speak, so my big brother and I were pretty much viewed as good boys by comparison.

When I reached my teenage years, for example, I don't remember my parents ever telling me I couldn't drink alcohol. I guess it was a given to them that I was going to go out with friends after football games and on weekends and have a couple of beers. But my parents did make it known that I was never to drink and drive. It was as though they had conceded that I was going to drink, so the best thing they could do for me was to put some regulations in place that would keep me safe.

My mind-set was that as long as I did good things—and "good things" sometimes meant nothing more than not doing some of the bad things that I knew others were doing—I was in good shape.

Our family went to a Catholic church every Sunday. There was never any question about whether we would attend Mass. My parents said we were going, and I did what I was told because I was an obedient kid, although I now realize that going to Mass was merely something I did because my parents went. For me, there never was any kind of sincere consideration of spirituality or a relationship with God.

We ate dinner together as a family and said our Catholic

Come From military Family [handwritten]

blessings over the food. As long as I did the good things associated with religion, I thought I was in good shape spiritually too. I thought doing the sacraments made me a Christian. I was an altar boy, went to my First Confession, and made First Communion. I even attended Catholic school through fifth grade. *Altar boy* [handwritten]

Obedience to authority was probably the main motivator of behavior in our home. With my dad's military background, he was accustomed to giving orders and having them followed. He expected obedience out of us, and we had grown up watching others — adults — obey his orders. More than that, we watched our dad obey the orders of his superiors. We saw obedience modeled every day.

When one of our parents became upset, hearing a curse word or two wasn't a surprise. They didn't cuss like sailors, as the saying goes, but there was never any talk afterward on their parts to steer us away from using such language. "Sin" wasn't a word used around our house. The Lord wasn't referenced as a way of letting one of us know that we had done something wrong. In our home, wrong was wrong, not because it was sin, but only because it was disobedience to our parents.

Never in the church, at Catholic school, or at home did I hear that I needed to become saved and accept Jesus Christ as Lord and Savior. Perhaps it was said somewhere along the way and I had missed it. I had heard of people becoming "born again," but I didn't know what it meant and only thought about it in terms of some type of strange, almost fanatic religious-cult type of experience. I never cracked open a Bible and read where Jesus clearly said, "you must be born again" to enter the kingdom of God.[1] I was in Mass every Sunday, I was doing everything I was supposed to at church, and outside of church I was getting into less trouble than a lot of my peers. So as far as I knew, I was good. *Not much religion* [handwritten]

Well, I eventually found trouble. And lots of it.

My parents may not have had many rules for us, but they did have some in place. Once I moved out on my own for college and it

---

1   See John 3:1–3.

Fred Behrend

was up to me to set the limits, there were even fewer rules, and I began getting into things I shouldn't have.

I was bitten by the wrestling bug at age twelve. During my senior year in high school, my dad made a connection and set up a meeting with Fred Behrend, who promoted matches for World Class Championship Wrestling. Fred informed me that I would need to be at least nineteen years old to obtain a wrestling license in Texas and said he would keep me in mind and give me a tryout after I finished college.

College wasn't my thing. I attended Southwest Texas State (now Texas State) for two semesters, but all I wanted to be was a wrestler. I took a speech communications class with the express purpose of learning speaking skills that would help me cut wrestling promos.

I had a 1.4 GPA my first semester, and when I told my dad that my only interest was in becoming a wrestler, he struck a deal with me: If I made a 2.5 my second semester, he would arrange another meeting with Fred Behrend. I made my 2.5, but only by a technicality. I officially pulled another 1.4, but if you erased the "F" for a class I thought I had dropped, my GPA came out to 2.5. Fortunately, that was enough for Dad to take me back to Mr. Behrend.

With Dad taking out a three-thousand-dollar loan to pay for my training, Mr. Behrend set me up to work with veteran wrestler Jose Lothario. In addition to teaching me the back flip, Jose proposed my ring name: Shawn Michaels. At first, I wasn't crazy about it. My real name is Michael Shawn Hickenbottom, and I had always gone by Shawn because I didn't like the name Michael. I was about to enter what I considered a bigger-than-life business, and I couldn't see "Shawn Michaels" generating any excitement. Since I had been called Shawn all my life, it seemed very normal, just a basic name. But I went along with Jose's idea because I wasn't able to come up with a better name.

I trained about three months with Jose before he arranged for my chance to break into the business, wrestling my first match for "Cowboy" Bill Watts's Mid-South Wrestling. I quickly discovered the demands of the wrestling schedule, as I took part in seven-to-nine shows a week, including doubles on weekends.

From Mid-South, I moved on to Central States Wrestling in Kansas City. It was there that I discovered the wrestler's lifestyle. Even though I was only nineteen, I began going out drinking with other wrestlers after matches. That was the beginning of a long slide into losing control of my life.

I am condensing here what is detailed in my first book, but as I began to grow in fame and stature, and as the aches and pains of our sport began to take over my body, I began to drink more and started taking drugs and pills and chasing women.

You name it, I tried it. And most of what I tried I kept doing.

The worse my lifestyle became, the more difficult I became to work with. It's fair to say that I was a jerk to many people in the business. But one thing I will say: All the partying *never* affected my ability to put on a good show in the ring.

Shawn Michaels—a fun-loving guy beginning to buy in to the rock-star attitude—became a shooting star, but Shawn Hickenbottom—once a pretty decent guy raised to be incredibly boring by comparison—was gradually fizzling out.

Fast-forward to 1998. I was watching the Monday night *Nitro* program of World Championship Wrestling (WCW) because I liked to see how friends in wrestling's other major organization were doing. Plus, it was always good to keep tabs on what the competition was up to.

Nitro featured dancers called the Nitro Girls. One in particular, who went by the name Whisper, stood out. I was telling a friend, Rich Minzer, about the dancer on television who had just about knocked my socks off. Rich ran a gym in California that wrestlers liked to visit when they were in his area, and a couple of weeks later he called to tell me that WCW was in town and that he had seen Whisper—and that she looked even better in person than she did on TV! I found that

Crush on Whisper – Rebecca Curci *WCW*

difficult to believe, but when Rich asked if I wanted him to try to get Whisper's phone number for me, that was one of the easiest questions I've ever answered. It took a little convincing and the help of another Nitro Girl, but Rich got me the phone number of Rebecca Curci.

Too nervous to call?

I was reluctant to call Rebecca because I felt like a stalker. After a couple of days, Rich called and said he had received a voice mail from Rebecca saying that she hadn't heard from me and she guessed it wasn't meant to be. Only then did I get up the nerve to call her.

The funny thing was that even though Rebecca was part of *Nitro*, she wasn't a fan of wrestling and had no idea who I was. Likely because I felt nothing like the Shawn Michaels character on TV who was brash and supremely confident around girls, I liked that.

We talked every night on the phone for two weeks. A few weeks later, Rebecca flew from her home in Atlanta to meet me in San Antonio. When she walked through the airport gate, I agreed with Rich's assessment: She did look more stunning in person. Our first visit together went great. We met again a few weeks later in Los Angeles.

Falls in Love

I knew then that I had found the one for me. I had fallen in love with Rebecca the first time I met her and knew that I would never meet anyone else who could be a friend to me like her, because she was fun to be around and not hesitant in the least to get playfully silly. She was extremely funny and made me laugh, and those were the type of people I tended to gravitate toward. Surprisingly for someone who played a dancer on television, she was humble and didn't carry herself like the unbelievably beautiful woman that she was. She was a traditional type of woman who enjoyed staying home and cooking. In many ways, we both were different in real life than who we were on television.

When I told family members and close friends that I wanted to marry Rebecca, I think all of them became concerned that I was rushing into the marriage. Everyone who met Rebecca absolutely loved her, so who I wanted to marry wasn't the problem. My mom expressed the most concern because of the place I was at in my life then. I hadn't exactly been the bastion of good judgment. She wanted me to spend

Mom suspect about me getting married

wanted to marry
Rebecca — Too soon?

more time getting to know Rebecca, to make sure that Rebecca's intentions were as pure as they appeared. Although my family and friends were supportive of me being with Rebecca, they weren't supportive of us marrying yet. Their opinions weren't going to sway me, however.

Three weeks after our time together in Los Angeles, with an Elvis impersonator as our witness, we married at the Graceland Wedding Chapel in Las Vegas.

Vegas Elvis wedding

Rebecca grew up Southern Baptist, and she was an example of someone who was raised in faith, fell away from it, came back to faith, and then would fall away again. I sensed that when we married, her spirituality meter was climbing. There were certain ministers whom she liked to watch on television, and she was doing her best to walk out her faith in a business that certainly didn't make that easy.

During our very first conversation, she had asked me, "Do you believe in Jesus?"

Believe?

"Yes," I quickly answered. "I'm Catholic."

Rebecca has since told me that the question she should have asked was, "Do you *know* Jesus?" That's a much different question. And it would have elicited a much different answer.

Of course I believe in Jesus, I told her. I had gone to church every Sunday growing up, but I did not *know* Jesus.

It didn't take long into our marriage for Rebecca to observe that.

It also didn't take long for a big change to occur. We had planned on starting a family soon after we married, but not as soon as we did. Six weeks after the wedding, Rebecca learned she was pregnant.

Pregnant in 6 weeks

That's the period of my life when, with two bad knees, a really bad back, and a hurting shoulder, I was taking thirty-to-thirty-five pills per day. I took them first thing in the morning, during the afternoon, and then again at night. I was a mess, often passing out on the couch. Rebecca would take care of me, making sure I was in a comfortable position for my back, and then go off to our bedroom and pray that God would help me stop the pills. When my mind was clear, she would tell me how much she hated going to bed alone and how much she missed her husband.

Pills

addicted to pain killers

"I'll stop when our baby is born," I promised her.

Cameron was born in January 2000, and there was nothing I wanted more than to be a good father to him. I cut back on the pills, but I didn't stop.

Cam born 2000 (margin note)

Rebecca had made significant changes in her life. I think that learning that she would be a mother motivated her to get back to her faith roots. She persistently prayed that I would make changes too. Then when Cameron was about nine months old and I was still living in my old ways, she sat me down and told me she loved me, but that for Cameron's sake, she would leave me if I didn't change. She left that night with Cameron to stay at a hotel and leave me alone to think.

Threatened to Leave (margin note)

The next day she came back home and reminded me that she loved me and knew that I loved her, informed me that she had not really been who she wanted to be in front of me, and told me that she needed to make her faith a priority.

Rebecca began taking part in a Bible study, which I was fine with because I wanted to be a supportive husband. I definitely had my shortcomings, but I loved Rebecca more than I could imagine loving anyone, and I always wanted to support her. I took note of the differences I began seeing in Rebecca, especially how at peace she seemed.

Even though she had always told me she loved me and backed that up by consistently showing me that she loved me, I knew I could not have been easy to live with. It wasn't that she started overlooking my pill-popping and passing out on the couch; instead, it seemed as if she had gained a renewed hope that I could change and that it would not be up to her to make it happen.

I had no plans of going down the path of faith Rebecca had chosen, but I was genuinely happy for her. Plus, it made me feel good about myself that I was being supportive of Rebecca's spiritual pursuits. Frankly, at that point, I needed some things I could pat myself on the back for.

One day I shared with Rebecca that I thought it would do me

some good to read the Bible, but that its old language—all the *ye's* and *thee's*—made it difficult for me to understand. For Christmas, she gave me a Bible written in a more contemporary language, the New Living Translation Study Bible. The language was simple and made more sense to me than what I had tried to read growing up, and the accompanying study notes at the bottoms of the pages helped me better understand the meanings behind the Scriptures.

She also gave me a couple of books that Christmas, and one of them really had a major impact on me. James Dobson's *Straight Talk to Men* was the first book I had read that clearly defined from a biblical perspective what was expected of a husband and a father. The book challenged me to be a strong leader in my family.

As I read through Dr. Dobson's book, I recognized all the areas where I was falling incredibly short of what I needed to be. None of what was expected of a real man seemed overtly soft, either. The book never made my role sound as if I needed to be a wishy-washy, goody-two-shoes type of Christian guy. I was a wrestler. I was into *tough*, and it felt as if the book was throwing down the gauntlet on my manhood. That was important because I wanted to be a good husband to Rebecca. I also wanted to be a good father to our son. I loved them both and wanted to provide for them the best I could, and the realization that I was failing to do so bothered me deeply.

Another book that greatly affected me was an outdoors survival guide. It was a small, almost underground type of book that my brother-in-law had picked up at a gun show and given to me. Because of the back injury that had forced me to retire from the ring, I was making only a few appearances with WWE then. Vince was good to me, doing me a favor by using me here and there in a referee's role or as a special commissioner. Being out from under the busy schedule of wrestling, for the first time I had the opportunity to explore hobbies and develop other interests, and I began getting interested in the outdoors.

At the beginning of the book, the author wrote that he was a Christian and that if his readers did not have Christ in their lives, they would not be good at following the tips and advice he would be sharing in the book.

That book was fresh on my mind when I took my first hunting trip, excited to finally have the time to do the hunting that I had been wanting to do for a long time. I was sitting alone in a deer blind, probably halfway incoherent because of heavens-knows-what I had taken before I got into the blind, and watching the stars fade as the sun rose to signal the opening of a crisp, fall morning in the Texas Hill Country. It's difficult to explain, but it was a kind of serene scene that gave me the opportunity to decompress. Even now, I can't really point to what specifically impacted me in that deer blind, but it was a spiritual moment such as I had never experienced before.

I had wanted our son to grow up in church, because I knew from my childhood that church was a good influence on a family. More importantly, because of what I was reading in the Bible and other books, it was becoming increasingly important that *I* attend church. My parents had instilled in me and my siblings that the church was where you could go when everything fell apart. Thus I knew that there was something I needed in my life, and I would probably find it in the church before I found it anywhere else. I definitely hadn't found it in any of the other places I had been.

It strikes me that even though I had grown up in church without actually being aware of what it truly was, all those years later the church became a magnet drawing me back to where I needed to be.

Church became like the note on a fire extinguisher in a hotel hallway: "In case of emergency, break glass." No, I don't consider faith an emergency-only option, because it is much more than that. But I recognized that my life had reached emergency status. My situation called for breaking the glass.

We started going back to my Catholic church, but Rebecca didn't like it there and said she thought we needed to find another church. I asked where she wanted to go, and she suggested we try Cornerstone Church. It was near our home, and Rebecca had watched the pastor, John Hagee, on television when she lived in Atlanta.

I wasn't excited about going to a "TV church," but, again, aware that I had an opportunity to pat myself on the back for being a supportive husband, I said we could go to Cornerstone. At least Cornerstone was close to where we lived, so if it turned out to be what I expected, it wouldn't have put me out too much.

Our first visit was on Father's Day, and we had Cameron with us in the service. I guess he was moving around or making noises or something, because the woman sitting in front of us kept turning around and giving us this mean look. That turned me off to the church.

They're just snobs here, I thought.

After the service, I told Rebecca we could scratch that church off our list. The next Sunday, we went back to my church, but Rebecca again told me she wasn't happy there. We agreed to look for another church to try.

While trying to find a church to attend regularly, reading the Bible that Rebecca had given me and some books on fatherhood motivated me to cut my pill-popping to only Friday nights. I hadn't quit, but I did feel that I was taking determined steps in the right direction.

One day in April 2002, I was driving around with Cameron in his car seat and, without realizing where I was, pulled to a stop in the Cornerstone parking lot.

"What are we doing, Daddy?" he asked.

"I don't know, son. We are just sitting here."

My cell phone rang just then, and when the call ended, I set out to finish our errands and return home. I relayed to Rebecca about stopping in the church parking lot for no apparent reason and that I felt that, based on what I had noticed take place in her life, I needed to find a Bible study I could belong to.

The next day I returned to Cornerstone, parked the car, walked into the church office, and told the lady at the front desk, "I am looking for a Bible study."

I later learned that one of the pastors heard me from his office,

43

Keith Parker

recognized me as Shawn Michaels, and was suspicious that I had come into the church as some kind of wrestling story for television.

One pastor did come out of his office and introduced himself as Keith Parker.

"You can come to my Bible study," he offered in a thick, Southern drawl. Keith gave me his address and told me to be there at 7:30 the next night.

When I arrived at Keith's home a little before the start of the Bible study, his wife, Priscilla, and a couple of other people were there. Keith asked if I was a Christian.

"No," I said. "I was raised Catholic, though."

"Have you ever been born again?" he asked.

"No, I was born just the one time that I know of," I answered.

"Would you like to accept Jesus Christ as your Lord and personal Savior?" Keith asked.

"Yes, I would."

"Have you ever said the Sinner's Prayer?" he asked.

accepts Jesus I spun through my mental Rolodex of Catholic prayers I had said and didn't come across that one. Keith then led me in the prayer, and I wept like a baby.

Sinners prayer I could feel what I've heard others describe about the moment they accepted their salvation: It was like burdens were falling off of me and chains were being loosened. Up to that point I had been sensing numerous changes taking place within me. But still I had felt like there was one thing more I needed, even though I couldn't identify what it was. After saying that prayer, I knew that salvation was what had been missing.

I drove home quickly after the Bible study, all excited to share what had happened with Rebecca.

"Oh my goodness, it's Jesus!" I told her when I walked through the door. "I confessed Him as Lord and Savior!"

Rebecca smiled and said she knew all along that Jesus was who I needed in my life.

"But you needed to come about it on your own," she added. "I didn't want to force you. I didn't want to push you."

Keith had told me at the Bible study that the next step for me *Baptist* would be to get baptized in water as a public proclamation that I had accepted Jesus as my Lord and Savior. A couple of weeks later, that took place. I came out of that water feeling very different on the inside. One of the interesting things for me in taking that public step is that I was still Shawn Michaels to a lot of people. It was a humbling process for me to go through the baptism in front of people, and I believe that God honored my obedience to Him. I've wondered whether being a public figure had kept me from humbling myself to take some of the obedient steps I had been needing to take for many years.

I'm thankful that I had a wife who was praying for me.

Throughout the entire time leading up to the night I went to that Bible study, Rebecca had never nagged me. But neither had she stuck her head in the sand, oblivious to the circumstances. As much as she had every right to nag me into changing my ways, she hadn't. Instead, she showed me love, she let the transformation in her life serve as an example for me, and more important, she faithfully and persistently prayed for me.

I'm telling you, *that* is a loving and godly wife, and I will forever be grateful for Rebecca.

April 2002
becomes a Christian

CHAPTER 3
THE GIFT OF WRESTLING

"The world and its desires pass away, but whoever does the will of God lives forever" (1 John 2:17).

I became a Christian in April 2002, a little more than four years after injuries forced me to retire following the Steve Austin match. I made TV appearances for WWE for a little more than a year before dropping off the national wrestling scene.

During that time away, Vince had called me up to headquarters in Stamford, Connecticut, because he wanted to bring me back as an on-air personality. I explained to Vince that I felt strongly that God was working on something in my life and that I was afraid of missing *WWE* what He was trying to tell me. I declined Vince's offer, telling him *announcer* that I didn't think it was a good idea for me at the time.

I had previously called Vince shortly after I got saved and baptized, told him that I had become a Christian, and added that if he *Called Vince* needed me to return to WWE, I would like to come back and help. Vince said he didn't have anything for me at that time but would want me back when there was a spot. About a month later, he called to tell me that he had found a place for me to work as an on-air character.

Even though I had told him I wanted to work at WWE again, I wasn't sure if I should, because so many changes had taken place

47

in my life since I had left, including the double life-changing events of having a son and getting saved. My outlook on everything had changed 100 percent. As a new Christian, I was hyper-aware of my new status and feeling that I was not supposed to do anything that would be considered remotely suspect for a Christian. I was unsure how I could go back into a line of work where everything would end up in a fight, even if for me it was just playing a part. It intimidated me to think of trying to make those two worlds—being a wrestler and a Christian—co-exist. But then again, as a new Christian I was on fire for the Lord and felt that there was something I needed to be doing for Him. I just didn't know what that something was. *Perhaps,* I wondered, *I should try to get involved with a ministry instead of wrestling.*

I had quickly made friends in my Bible study and in the church, so I began asking some of them for advice. As helpful as they were to me in beginning my Christian walk, none of them could give me the specific answer I was looking for. On the one hand, they could see that I wanted to do something public with my Christianity and that wrestling offered an unbelievably large platform. On the other hand, because WWE had a black eye image-wise, some expressed concerns about me returning to wrestling and facing temptations from the lifestyle I had been living. I know what the public perception of WWE is, and I understand some of why it is that way, but WWE is far from the den of evil it is portrayed to be. I think that stigma could be why my friends couldn't provide a clear answer as to what I should do.

The typical answer was "Pray about it, brother." Now, let me say that "Pray about it" is probably the best advice we can give anyone facing any kind of decision. So I don't want to come across as saying that's not a good answer. It should be a part of every answer. But what I experienced as a very new Christian was that praying about it presented some difficulties for me. Mainly, I knew how to pray, but I didn't know how I would hear God's answer, especially to a question as specific as "Do I take this job or not?"

How would God let me know? Would I hear a voice? Would I

walk out my front door and see a skywriter leaving a "Yes" or "No" in the sky? Would someone hear God's voice and give me the answer? And if the latter was the case, why were some Christians I trusted telling me I should go back to WWE and others were telling me I shouldn't?

I would go to my gym and pray there, sometimes lying on the floor and trying to be still and quiet. I would listen to Christian music, hoping I would feel something that would lead me to the answer. Nothing produced an answer.

Until one Sunday when I was in church and my cell phone rang. *Bruce*

It was Bruce Pritchard, a producer with WWE. I stepped out *Pritchard* into the lobby and answered. Bruce asked if I could make it to *Raw* the next night. I said that I was in church and would have to call him back.

Almost as soon as I had returned to my seat, Pastor Hagee said in his message that we can seek out wise counsel when we need guid- *Pastor* ance, but at the same time we could ask ten different Christians a *Hagee* question and get ten different answers. Boy, had I already learned that. But, Pastor Hagee continued, we should faithfully pray and God will answer our prayer. That's the part I was struggling with. But then he added that God will always let us know what He wants us to do.

God will let you know.

I immediately thought about Bruce's call and wondered what the chances were that he would call with that question during church *said* and right before Pastor Hagee would make that statement. *Yes*

After church, I talked with Rebecca about Bruce's offer and what Pastor Hagee had said.

"It's up to you," she said.

I called Bruce and told him I would be there the next day.

I didn't have to walk in the door and shout, "I'm a Christian now!" A few months earlier, I had taken part in an interview with part of the WWE media in which one of the main topics was the

Montreal Screwjob—one of the biggest controversies ever in wrestling, which I just so happened to be squarely in the middle of.

In 1997, Bret Hart was leaving WWE for WCW. I was to be Bret's opponent for his final match which, to complicate matters for Vince's plan that Bret drop his WWF Champion title on the way out, would take place in Canada, Bret's home country. Leading up to the match, Bret had made it known that he would not give up the belt if he had to give it to me. (We already had a fierce rivalry in place before all this happened.)

Vince arranged for what is known in the business as a "swerve," or secretly setting up a match to turn out different from the prearranged result. Bret didn't know what was coming, and when I defeated him to take his belt away in front of his fellow countrymen, he understandably became enraged. When he left for WCW, we didn't exchange a single word for more than a decade, he took every opportunity to bash me and WWE publicly, and the Montreal Screwjob became the most hotly discussed topic in wrestling for years.

In creating the swerve, Vince had told me to say I did not know it would happen because he wanted to take responsibility for it and try to keep my name clean in connection with the situation. That's what I had done for all those years. But in my newfound status as a Christian, I didn't want to lie. So when I was asked in that interview about the Montreal Screwjob, I said, "I don't know if you guys know this, but I knew it was going down."

Judging by the shocked expression on the interviewer's face, I would say she didn't know!

"Vince told me adamantly that I was never to talk about that," I continued, "because he wanted to take responsibility for it. I'm not comfortable with that anymore. Can I just say it?"

The interviewer—remember, she worked for WWE—seemed confused and said she didn't know what to do and would have to ask headquarters.

We stopped the interview, and I called Vince, but he didn't

answer his phone. So I told the interviewer, "I am just going to tell you the truth, and I will let you guys edit it out if you need to."

I then gave her the scoop on the Montreal Screwjob, and they ended up airing that part of the interview. Revealing the complete truth about what had taken place obviously made big news, and my faith came out as the reason for my finally telling the true story.

So when I did return to WWE to be a part of *Raw*, my being a Christian was well known.

In the four-plus years I had been gone, there had been a good amount of turnover among the wrestlers. But the ones still there who had wrestled with me — the ones who had been eyewitnesses to many of my old ways — said they noticed a complete change in me right away.

The first time I saw Kevin Nash, whom I used to go out with and drink a case of beer with almost every night, he told me he could tell that I had come out of the water when I was baptized as "a different man." Kevin would have supported me no matter what, but he could tell that I was a new man.

Everyone at WWE was so welcoming of me and accepting of my Christianity, all the way up to Vince. I would say that most of the guys appeared thrilled for me. I knew there would be some who wondered if my change was for real — after all, we all worked in a business that relied on coming up with creative storylines — and if my new way of living would last.

No one, including me, knew how long I would be back with WWE. I had undergone surgery to fuse my back at the L4 and L5 vertebrae and create more space between the L5 and S1. The surgeon also took a piece of my hip and placed it between the L4 and L5, then screwed everything together using a metal plate.

While I considered it a miracle from God that I could even consider wrestling again, much less do so, there was no commitment from either side for anything beyond that one match. I wanted to see how my back would respond, and WWE had no interest in pushing me beyond that.

51

The uncertainty of how long I would be with WWE again put a sense of urgency in my wanting to be a good witness. I felt that God had brought me back to that platform to do something positive for Him, and I did not want to waste the one opportunity I knew I could count on. I didn't become a Bible-thumper, getting in guys' faces and demanding to know where they stood with the Lord. But I knew that they expected me to be different, and I wanted to show them that the changes in me were real and lasting, that what God had done in my life was legit, and that He could make the same difference in their lives.

In my earlier days in wrestling, I hadn't known how many Christians there were among the guys. First, I wasn't interested in knowing who was a believer. Second, the Christians, trust me, would not have been spending their free time where I was hanging out. Third, in the wrestling environment I was brought into as a youngster, we talked very little about our personal lives. There was this handed-down understanding that wrestlers did not let anyone else in the locker room see their weaknesses. It was like we were on guard all the time, dedicated to concealing any vulnerability. We wore tough-guy masks around each other because we were wrestlers.

When I returned in 2002, I was surprised at the shift in the locker-room culture. While it wasn't a completely new environment, there still had been enough of a transformation that guys could show insecurity or fear. It wasn't a bad thing anymore to admit that a situation intimidated you. This all probably came along as part of the changes of that era in wrestling as an industry.

Whatever the reason, guys felt free to come up and tell me about their faith, and I don't believe that would have occurred before my retirement. I have to say that there were a few guys who really surprised me when they told me about their faith. I'm not the judgmental type, but I would not have expected to hear from some that they had experienced salvation at some point in their lives.

Kevin, my drinking buddy whom I knew about as well as any of the wrestlers, told me he had attended Fellowship of Christian

Athlete meetings when he had played basketball at the University of Tennessee back in the late 1970s.

"Really?" I asked him. "How come you never said anything about it?"

"With the life we were living?" he replied. "Are you kidding me?"

I laughed, because I understood his point.

Chris Jericho, who had moved into WWE from WCW while I was away, was a Christian. We would pray with each other before matches. There was a six-man Elimination Chamber match out in Phoenix that Kevin, Jericho, and I were in, and the three of us were getting ready to pray before going out to the ring. Hunter, whom I had never known to make any profession of faith, joined us. Then while we were praying, Bill Goldberg came over, put his big arms around us, and prayed with us.

Just as I don't judge anyone, I also don't try to claim that because someone takes part in a prayer he is automatically a Christian. But here were all these guys about to get into the ring together for a match, and they were coming together to pray at least for a moment in time, and the Lord was being glorified in that moment. To be able to look back on occasions like those and know that I had not previously seen such displays in wrestling provides special memories for me even now.

When I returned to WWE, I became the "resident Christian" that guys could come and talk to whenever they had spiritual questions or were dealing with tough situations. Perhaps I was partly a token Christian, but heck, that was all right with me. That wasn't such a bad gig. The way I saw it, at least they knew I was a guy they could go to because they could see that my faith was real and that I had a little insight to the Christian life.

That was a time when we experienced far too many wrestlers dying far too young, and there were guys who would seek me out to talk whom I could tell had been suddenly forced to consider their own mortality. I would share what my faith had done in my life and answer whatever questions of theirs that I could.

In 2005 Eddie Guerrero died in a hotel room from what was later determined to be a heart attack. I called Vince to let him know, and Hunter and I were allowed to go up onto the same floor as Eddie's room. That happened on a Monday, and we had a *Raw* to shoot that night. In wrestling, the show always goes on as scheduled. While we were planning to make that night's *Raw* a tribute to Eddie, Vince told me, "I talk to God, but I do it in my own way."

"That's all right," I told Vince. "Different guys communicate to Him in different ways."

"Well, look," he told me. "Eddie was a Christian like you. I'm just thinking about getting everybody together, and what do you think about saying a prayer?"

"That would be awesome," I told Vince. "I think that would mean a lot to Eddie to bring everybody together. I don't think that's ever been done around here."

"I pray in my own way," Vince said. "Do you mind doing the prayer?"

"I'd be honored."

"Okay," he said. "I'll get everybody together. We'll have a little meeting and let them know what is going on, what we are going to do for the show. And then I will just let everybody know that you are going to say a prayer and if they want to stay, they can. If not, they don't have to."

The more those types of opportunities arose and the more conversations I had with wrestlers that I knew would not have taken place in my earlier days, the more I believed that God had wanted me to go back to WWE, and for a reason.

The Christian friends who expressed hesitancy about me returning to wrestling did so out of concern for me. I have said that WWE is not as evil as it is often made out to be, but there obviously had been plenty of pitfalls there for me to fall into my first time around.

Rebecca might have experienced a little bit of trepidation, but when I asked her opinion about me returning, she said she was at peace with it. When I went back, my old lifestyle had absolutely no appeal to me. I didn't want to live in a way that would be detrimental to me or my family. For the first time in my life I felt that I could clearly see the lines between right and wrong.

My salvation came with the realization that if you don't live for something, you don't live for much of anything. My something was Jesus, my Lord and Savior, and I no longer wanted to maintain a lifestyle that would disappoint the One who had given His life for me.

With the change that God brought to my life, there was nothing about my previous lifestyle that I wanted to revisit for old times' sake.

The assumption was that before I became a Christian, I had fallen prey to the pursuit of fame and money associated with the wrestling lifestyle. Based on that assumption, I understood why some people were concerned about my going back to WWE. But the assumption was false.

Fame and money and those pursuits were not a temptation for me. They were not a threat for me. They were not the reasons I had gotten into all the stuff I had before. I had drunk a lot, done drugs, and popped pills for two reasons: because of boredom, and because I was empty and lonely. My wife used to say that idle hands are the devil's workshop, and that was true with me, because a lot of the destructive things I did were just a way to kill time.

Our schedules back then were so busy that all there really was time for outside of wrestling was sitting in a hotel room watching TV until you fell asleep. That, to me, was torture. Plus, I didn't like to be alone with myself, because I didn't like myself. I went out and drank because that was a way to be with others. I did drugs to get high and took pills to get relaxed so I could get into a mental state where I wouldn't have to deal with who I had become.

I never had any withdrawals once I quit. I found Jesus, and I was done with the drugs and pills. Just like that. I have had surgeries since and have had no problems getting off the pain pills after I recovered.

I took the pills exactly as prescribed and stopped exactly when I was supposed to.

To me, the complete life turnaround was the strongest witness I could have as a Christian. Although there were a lot of new faces in WWE, I knew they had heard stories about me. The biggest reputation black marks against me were being difficult to work with and being a pill head. While some of the old-timers who were still around might have wondered if the change would last, I think they also hoped I had changed for good, because they remembered quite well how I had been before, when I had been hanging out in the bars, drinking, doing drugs, messing around with women, going off on people, and generally being disrespectful.

When I had left the first time, the range of how much I was liked by the other wrestlers was probably little to none, with the exception of my best friend, Hunter. I guess one of the upsides to the hell of a life I had lived was that I had set the bar so low that it would not have taken much effort to not be as bad as what I had been. Trust me, that is not something to be proud of!

I used to be one of the guys going to the strip clubs. I didn't go to those places when I went back. Gosh, I didn't even know if the younger guys were going to them. I didn't know where they went. When I could, I brought my family with me. I did that so we could spend more time together, but one of the by-products was that the guys got to see me with my family and their mental images of me would be me with my family instead of in those other places. I think that simply not being seen in certain places I had previously frequented proved to be a pretty viable witness on its own.

I had only one fear associated with my return: that I would not be as good a wrestler as before. I didn't know how much my back could withstand, but I wasn't as worried about my body as much as I was my wrestling ability. I was thirty-seven years old when I got back into the ring at the *SummerSlam* pay-per-view event, working

an angle in which Triple H had turned on me. My knees and back felt
years older than thirty-seven, but the fans ate up the Triple H angle,
and when our match went over well and I didn't experience too much
unexpected soreness afterward, I was back to wrestling.

I didn't wrestle full-time, managing my schedule so I could spend
time at home and still be available for the run-up to and during the
big events.

The fans were receptive to the cleaned-up Shawn Michaels. I
knew I would face the same challenges with them that I did with the
guys. Namely, was this change real and would it last?

I couldn't blame the fans for being suspicious that the Christian story might be just another made-up wrestling storyline. In every
personal interview I took part in, I made sure to include my faith in
an effort to show that I had experienced a legitimate, real-life change.

I also started incorporating Christian words and symbols into
my wardrobe. I wore overt Christian T-shirts into the ring, such as
shirts that included Jesus' name or made a declaration such as "He Is
Risen." I was excited about the shirts, and I took a bit of heat from
fans for wearing them and for talking about God so openly. But I had
expected that and had determined I wasn't going to let it bother me.
I was genuinely happy and was telling folks long before I knew that
"I shouldn't."

Vince was fine with the messaged shirts, too, although he did
come to me after a couple of months of me wearing them and said he
wanted to ask a question about my shirts.

"Do you have a problem with them?" I asked Vince.

"I think they're great," he answered. "But there are some coun-
tries where we air that we have to digitally alter the overt Jesus stuff.
I'm not asking you to change what you're doing; I'm asking what we
can do."

Vince offered to have WWE create and merchandise shirts that
would be able to be aired unaltered in those places while still getting
out the message I wanted to send. He said it would be cheaper for

HBK w/ Christian symbols

WWE to make the shirts for me than to continue digitally altering them for certain locations.

I thought about it and agreed. That put the creative gurus at WWE in charge of my shirts, and they started designing me shirts with crosses on them and "HBK" (for Heartbreak Kid) inside an Ichthys, the Christian fish symbol.

Spending fifteen seconds in the ring before a match with a message on a T-shirt might not seem like having much impact until you realize that we were watched by four to five million people per week in just the United States. That was a big audience!

HBK religious symbol

As for what those people were watching in the ring, I believe a strong case can be made that despite the physical issues, I was a better wrestler—and certainly a better storyteller—in the second part of my career than in the first. Not bad for a dude who not only hadn't planned on ever wrestling again, but also had struggled with the decision as to whether he should even rejoin WWE.

I learned a valuable spiritual lesson in my return to wrestling: God does not give us gifts that He does not intend for us to use.

Even in the days when my life was out of control, I considered my wrestling abilities a gift from God. I say it humbly when I say that I could wrestle really well. It always came naturally to me. There was nothing about the job of wrestling itself that I did not like or would define as work. To me, digging a six-foot ditch is work. Hard work! But wrestling wasn't.

Being good at wrestling was never difficult for me. Someone once told me that God isn't a bait-and-switch kind of God, and I don't believe that God would have given me the gift of being a good wrestler and then not want me to wrestle.

The Lord built me to be a pro wrestler, and I did the best with what I had and tried to make the most use of my platform when I could. I would say that before my salvation, I wrestled because I had a God-given ability. Afterward, I wrestled because God had a purpose for me.

CHAPTER 4
GRATEFUL FOR SCARS

*"And the God of all grace, who called you to his eternal
glory in Christ,... will himself restore you and make
you strong, firm and steadfast" (1 Peter 5:10).*

I was having a conversation with a WWE camera guy named
Stu early in 2009 when he asked how old my son was.

"Nine," I said.

"He's halfway gone," he said.

"What do you mean?"

"He is halfway to eighteen, man," Stu said, "and then he's gone."

Holy cow, I said to myself, *time is flying!*

Then I thought back to the times when I had said I didn't want
to miss seeing Cameron and Cheyenne grow up and wanted to maintain an active presence in their lives. And it hit me that Cameron was
halfway gone. Stu's words made me want to be home even more.

That also happened to be during the toughest time we had gone
through as a family.

A few years earlier someone had approached me with the idea
of starting a business in San Antonio that would be one of those fun
places for kids to have birthday parties and the like. I mentioned it
to Rebecca, and she hadn't thought it a good idea. I did not give it
another thought. Rebecca, however, did. She prayed about it for a
while and began to feel that it was something we should do.

Opened a gym?

Blessed to be in a position where we could start and operate a business that kids could enjoy, including our own, we bought land, built a 20,000-square-foot building, and invested money in getting the business up and running. Our place did well for a couple of years, but with me still traveling on a regular basis, managing the business proved to be too much of a load for Rebecca with everything else she had going on, including homeschooling our children.

Rebecca is a strong, independent woman. When we met, she was supporting herself with her job as a Nitro Girl, and when we married, I wanted to take care of her in a way where she would not have to work. Rebecca pushed back at first, saying, "I don't need you taking care of me."

I told her it wasn't that I thought she *needed* me to take care of her; it was that I *wanted* to take care of her. Rebecca had a three-year contract with Nitro, and it took some work to get her out of the contract because Nitro suspected she was trying to join me at WWE. We had no such plans. After negotiations by lawyers, Nitro released Rebecca with the stipulation that she could not go to work for WWE for the duration of her contract.

As a sidebar, we once had to answer some background questions to work with a ministry for children. The guy helping us through the forms asked Rebecca what her job was and then made the mistake of adding, "If you're just a homemaker, you can put 'Homemaker' there." Rebecca didn't say anything but wrote down her job as "Homemaker, homeschool two children, handle taxes, pay bills, and take care of the enterprise that is Shawn Michaels." She definitely was not "just" a homemaker! Even as much as I already appreciated Rebecca, seeing that list on paper gave me more of a sense of what all she did for our family.

Running our business with my irregular help required more time and energy than she (or anyone in her situation) could afford, and although the business was doing well, maintaining it developed into a sour experience for the whole family. We closed the business in 2009

Closed the building in 2009

and put the building up for sale. Shortly after, we decided we wanted to move.

I had always wanted to own a ranch, and Rebecca and I had talked for several years about one day living on one. I would spend downtime looking on the Internet at ranches for sale, and one place that intrigued me kept popping up. But after the match against The Undertaker at *WrestleMania 25* and at the same time as our business closing made it possible for us to move from San Antonio, the place disappeared from among the ranches for sale.

We made the decision that I would retire the following year, and we put the house up for sale. We found another ranch we thought would be suitable, and then one day while I was looking through the real estate sites again, my dream ranch appeared back on the market. We visited our second choice and thought it was okay, but when we stepped onto the property of the one I had wanted all along, it was exactly what we were praying for.

Like Abraham, I packed up my tent and moved the family.

A funny thing about Christianity is you can make what someone else would call a dumb move, yet to a Christian it is considered a step of faith. Faith involves risk, and there was risk involved in our moving while having a home and the building from our business both up for sale. Plus, I knew retirement was coming and had no idea if I would have any income after that. Yes, I had made good money during my career, but even if you have had seven-figure contracts during your career, it is still scary to think about not having any contract. Hickenbottom men tend to worry over finances, and unfortunately for Rebecca, that family trait did not skip over me.

When I became a Christian, I learned that Christians are supposed to tithe—give 10 percent of their income to God as recognition that all we have comes from Him, and I wondered if it would be okay if we started out giving just 5 percent to see how it went. I completely understood that 10 percent is 10 percent no matter how

Gave 10% to the church [handwritten]

much money you have. Despite that, my 10 percent looked pretty big to me. God asks for 10 percent, though, and between Rebecca's persuasion and the Holy Spirit's conviction, God won out. He got His 10 percent. We trusted God and regularly gave the full tithe because, if you think about it, giving back 10 percent is a good deal in light of the fact that *everything* we have comes from God.

There was another time when Rebecca felt led to give a large amount of money beyond our tithe. A guest minister was speaking at Cornerstone. Our church was raising funds at the time to pay off debt, and this minister talked about how his church had done the same thing and, as a sign of his faith that God would meet our church's needs, announced that he was going to give a certain amount to our church.

I saw Rebecca reach for her checkbook. I leaned over to her and softly asked, "What makes me think you are going to match his check and we're going to give that much to the church?"

She turned to look me in the eyes and said, "Oh, we are going to beat him."

My first thought was, *Oh my goodness!*

"Is it okay?" she asked.

Dad handled it then Rebecca [handwritten]

I hadn't seen one of my paychecks in a gazillion years. I'm not good with numbers, and my dad used to handle all my finances for me. Then when I got married, Rebecca took care of our money and has been an excellent manager of our finances.

I trusted her and nodded for her to go ahead.

Rebecca wrote out the check and handed it to me. I looked at the amount, and let's just say we weren't only beating this minister's amount, but were lapping him two or three times!

Rebecca and I don't give money in church to make more money, as the "prosperity gospel" pattern of giving teaches. We tithe out of obedience to what God's Word instructs us. We give additional offerings, such as the one to help the church with its debt, when we feel that the Holy Spirit wants us to allow others to be blessed out of the blessings we receive. Not one cent we possess will leave this earth. We won't be able to take any of it with us when we die, but we do have the ability now to help serve God's purpose here through giving to missions and other causes.

So Rebecca and I determined to be faithful and obedient with our finances even when circumstances didn't make sense to us. We've learned through experience to trust God with our finances. He may not always give us what we want, but He *always* makes sure we have what we need, and that is plenty good for us.

It took two years for our home to sell, and we took a financial beating on that. As of this writing, the building from our business still has not sold, and that has been more than four years now. All that time it has been just sitting there, unused, and siphoning five figures a month out of our bank account.

That being said, I don't want to sound as though we were destitute. We bought a ranch, our home took two years to sell, and we have had a building for sale for four years and counting. That is a pretty good drain on one's money. But I also had done well financially during my career and, with my dad's help and Rebecca's, managed not to blow everything I made despite the lifestyle I had led.

I know that many people—especially men, based on the conversations I've had—have made decisions with business or money that they later regretted or became burdened with. But this is not a story about my finances. It is actually a story about God's faithfulness, because although I have stressed while watching money flow out in a steady stream, I also have been mindful of how God has provided for us. I learned a big lesson about trusting God and remaining obedient to Him.

The temptation for me was to keep wrestling to continue earning income. I am like most men in that the default solution in a difficult time, especially if it pertains to finances, is to work my way out of it. I could have worked out any deal I wanted with WWE. They would have paid me good money to wrestle only a few times a year.

Although I have been dropped on my head more than a few times in my life, even I could see that it would make sense to keep wrestling so I could make more money than we were losing. However, I didn't feel that was what God wanted me to do. He wanted me to be at home, so I stayed with the plan to retire and told God that I would trust Him on the finances.

I did not know what would happen when I retired, but before I was inducted into the WWE Hall of Fame in April 2011, Vince signed me to a ten-year contract to make television appearances as I saw fit with my schedule. I also landed an outdoors television show that will have completed its fourth season by the time this book releases. My son races Legends cars, which are five-eighths scale versions of NASCAR-type cars and race on shorter tracks. His sole sponsor is a company called "Dad." Anyone who has been a part of racing can attest that it is an obscenely expensive sport. Cheyenne, who wants to become a veterinarian, has been a key player in our acquiring more than twenty animals that we feed and take care of. The anticipated addition of horses and 4H goats won't be easy on the wallet either.

I have yet to have to go back into the ring to earn more money. (But if that building doesn't sell … just kidding, I think.) That's because God has provided for us through the family's extremely stressful time waiting on the building to sell.

The situation involving the business has been a good test of my faith, because Rebecca and I felt all along that opening it had been God-ordained. We still believe that. We prayed over the land, we prayed over the entire situation, and we dedicated the business to Him. We were obedient with our finances. I'm not by any stretch the greatest guy in the world, but I have made it a habit to wake up in the morning and spend quiet time with the Lord. I have been a faithful servant. I have studied God's Word and know that "the prayer of a righteous person is powerful and effective."[2]

That was the first time in my life that I had dotted every *i* and

---

2 James 5:16.

crossed every *t* and still got kicked in the gut. I went through a range of emotions, including anger and bitterness. I must admit that I had been under the impression that for every bad deed there was a negative consequence and for every act of obedience there was a blessing. However, I surely had a lot of acts of obedience that seemed to result in negative consequences.

The blessings did come, however. They just didn't come where I was looking for them or when I thought they should come. They came in God's timing and in places in which He chose to reveal them to me.

While continuing to pray, "Lord, it would be awesome if that building would sell," I remain convinced that God will keep providing for us until the market gets back into good shape and we can unload the building.

This has been an unbelievably huge growth moment for me. I would prefer not to go through another trial like this again, but I am glad I have been through it. I have confidence that by being dependent on God, I can get through a similar situation if another should come my way. I am certainly better equipped for life's trials now than I was before.

———

When I wrote my first book, I had been a Christian for a couple of years. Sometimes that's referred to as the *honeymoon* stage of Christianity. I like to say that during that season everything was rainbows and unicorns for me. My prayer back then — and I prayed this almost every day — was, "Don't ever let me stop feeling like this."

"This" was that spiritual high I was on, being on fire for the Lord. Everything was wonderful.

I was blessed to have mature Christians around me when I became a believer. New Christians need to get involved rather than sitting back to see what unfolds. I joined a good Bible study in my church that was under a great leader and consisted of really good people. That lasted for two or three years until Keith Parker and his

Keith Parker moved to Alabama

wife, Priscilla, moved from San Antonio back to their home state of Alabama. Then Cameron and I began attending a Bible Study Fellowship through BSF International, and later I began leading a Bible study for young men from single-parent homes.

Led Bible Study for young Men

The point is that I made a conscious effort to get involved, and that placed me within a network of caring people who were more experienced at this Christian thing than I was and helped guide me through the early steps of my new walk with Christ. I do not want to say that I couldn't have made it without the help of those people, because God could have just as easily created another route for me to follow, but I surely am grateful I had that group of Christians around me.

There were several who told me early on that I was in a honeymoon period and things wouldn't feel forever exactly as they did as a new Christian. They made sure I understood that tough times would hit and my faith would be tested. Thanks to them, I didn't expect becoming a Christian to make life a breeze. Good thing, too, because anyone who tells you that when you become a Christian life gets easy and stays easy is flat-out wrong.

Tough times did come, just like they do with a typical marriage: financial strains, raising children in a world that tells them anything that is godly is not cool, the natural ups and downs of a marital relationship. And while I would not say that the high I wanted to keep experiencing left, I will say that it took on a different form.

I can compare it to my marriage. I still love Rebecca, but our relationship is not what it was like at the beginning. We have gone through tough times, working through them together. In the process of life's battles, we've grown closer to each other because we have learned more about each other. We've each been wounded, and although those wounds have healed, they have left scars. Rebecca and I each have scars from the closing of our business, but they give us an appreciation for having gone through the trial together and remind us of how God remained faithful to us throughout.

It is the same with my wrestling injuries. Because of what I feel when I get out of bed each morning, I will never forget what I did for

Injuries

Suffering

a living. I have two knees and a shoulder that need to be replaced. I need a heating pad to loosen up my back in the morning. My knees make it hard to get moving on cold mornings. My physical pains go well beyond "discomfort," but I don't complain about any of that, except to Rebecca. I joke that she signed up for this, so she has to listen to me!

My body paid a price for being a wrestler, but the injuries were part of the process that made it possible for my family to be where we are now. The injuries are my battle scars, and they help me appreciate what I have today.

I think our relationship with God is similar to our relationships with other people. At the beginning, everything is new and nifty and cool, but there comes a time when the dynamics of the relationship begin to change and a Christian becomes more centered, more rational, and more aware that the walk with God is not a cakewalk. As that relationship deepens, as we mature more as Christians, we experience a different, deeper level of faith.

Peter writes about that in the New Testament when he tells of God bringing us through various trials until the time when Christ returns.

> In all this you greatly rejoice, though now for a little while
> you may have had to suffer grief in all kinds of trials. These
> have come so that the proven genuineness of your faith — of
> greater worth than gold, which perishes even though refined
> by fire — may result in praise, glory and honor when Jesus
> Christ is revealed (1 Peter 1:6 – 7).

Although I have enjoyed the high of rainbows and unicorns and have suffered painful battle wounds, I would not trade anything for my scars because they remind me of how faithful God has been to me.

Chapter 5
Leaving a Legacy

"The heavens declare the glory of God; the skies proclaim the work of his hands" (Psalm 19:1).

I built my early wrestling name as an athletic wrestler who flew all around the ring and jumped off ladders and top ropes. Yet Keith Mark can tell enough stories about my bumbling ways to shoot down that reputation.

For the past four years, Keith and I have co-hosted the outdoors show *MacMillan River Adventures* on the Outdoor Channel. *[handwritten: T.V. Show]* The reputation I've earned there is as someone who has a tendency to fall into creeks and rivers. Fortunately, most of those bloopers don't make it onto the program. If a good friend is someone who is willing to overlook your faults, then where my outdoors clumsiness is concerned, Keith is a *great* friend.

I didn't think it possible that I would make such a close friend in my forties, but that is what Keith has become for me. Not only has he become my buddy, but he also is a strong Christian. Keith is different from me in that he has been a good dude his entire life. But Keith also is enough off his rocker that he has qualities like the guys I used to connect with in wrestling.

During my first retirement was the first time since getting into wrestling that I had been able to pursue a hobby. After reading the

[handwritten: Started as a hobby]

outdoors book by the Christian author, I dove into hunting, and when I was back in wrestling, I would watch the Outdoor Channel on my days off and think that having my own outdoors show could be a fun "job" after I retired for good.

Hunter knew how heavily I had gotten into the outdoors, and I think he was the only wrestler who knew about my hobby. When I would rejoin the guys after spending time at home, he would joke, "The more you are home, the more redneck you become."

One of those times when I was at home, I was recovering from a knee injury when WWE came on TV one night. John Cena got hurt, and Rebecca told me, "I guarantee you they will call you tomorrow."

She was correct.

"Can you come back early?" was the predictable question.

"My knee has another week or two to heal," I said.

"We don't need you to do much. Obviously, we will need you for the pay-per-view. We will get you in there with Randy Orton on *Raw*, and we'll take care of you."

Nearing the end of my career, I didn't think there was any more damage that could be done to my body. It already felt like everything had either fallen off or was tearing away, so I said I would hop on a plane and be there.

I was wearing boots, a cowboy hat, and a camouflaged vest when Vince saw me.

"What are you wearing tonight?" he asked.

"You're looking at it."

"No, you are not wearing that," Vince told me.

"Yes, I am," I responded.

(Just because I was a Christian didn't mean I couldn't still enjoy pushing Vince's buttons on occasion.)

"No," Vince said. "Not that."

"Look, I don't have anything else," I told him. "This is what I brought. You called me. I am wearing this."

"Not that," he said again.

"Let me tell you something," I said. "You called me. I have two more weeks to heal this knee. I can wear this, or I can go to the airport and go home."

"We'll talk about it," Vince finally said.

Randy and I set up how the Run-In would play out, and then Vince and I went to his office.

"What was that?" I asked. "You are dressing me down in front of everybody, and you ought to know by now that I'm not going to give. This is what I'm wearing."

"You can't wear that hat," Vince said.

"Yes, I can. It's a cowboy hat. I realize that in Stamford, Connecticut, you may not recognize what a cowboy hat is, but there is a whole world out there that does. I'm going to wear the hat. And I'm wearing this other stuff too. I'm not going to argue about it."

Argued over cowboy hat!

"Well," Vince replied, "you don't have to get upset."

"Get upset? You are giving me a hard time about what I'm wearing. And you do it in front of my peers. I'm not upset, but I don't like you dressing me down like that. If you don't like the way I dress, that's fine. I don't like the way you dress, but I don't tell you anything about it."

"Is this how it is going to be?" he asked.

"Yes, this is how it's going to be."

"All right," Vince said, and I went to the ring in my camouflaged vest and cowboy hat.

Within two weeks, WWE was selling Heartbreak Kid cowboy hats.

Sold hats

"The hats are growing on me," Vince told me.

With my interest in hunting out there for all of the wrestling world to see, one of our WWE camera guys told me he knew someone at the Outdoor Channel and offered to set up a meeting with him. That is when Rebecca and I met Keith, whom I had watched on television. A couple of weeks after our meeting, Keith called to talk and we hit it off right away. He had previously hosted the *MacMillan River Adventures* show and invited me on a hunt for a guest appearance on the new version of the show.

Gets on Outdoor Channel meets Keith Mark

Goes on a hunt

Keith took me on a bison hunt in North Dakota on the Standing Rock Sioux Reservation. I shot a bison with a muzzleloader, and it was a surreal and spiritual moment sharing that experience with the Sioux because it was a big deal for them to allow us to come onto their reservation and hunt.

During the trip we were talking in one of our hotel rooms, and the conversation led to personal topics such as family. Keith and I began to find out how much we have in common. Our core values were the same, and we both loved being in the outdoors for what we believed were the right reasons. I thought it was amazing to be able to have a talk with that kind of openness and honesty with another guy on a hunting trip.

post-wrestling career

The trip was supposed to be a one-time hunt, but I shared with Keith that I had an interest in working on an outdoors show after wrestling, yet knew nothing about the business.

Keith presented the idea of the two of us working together. He had the experience and said I would bring in a new group of viewers. I prayed about it, and that answer was a little easier to receive than when I had prayed about whether I should return to WWE! I was offered a contract with the *MacMillan River Adventures* show and a really, really close friend. Neither Keith nor I consider it coincidence that we wound up working together.

My entry into outdoors television came like the other events in my life that have impacted me the most: When presented with an opportunity, I jumped right in. For about ten years before I joined the show, I'd had limited time for hunting. I loved hunting, but with my wrestling schedule, I just hadn't had the chance to make more than an occasional hunting trip. Over those ten years, I'd hunted probably the equivalent of only two seasons, primarily in the fall for white-tailed deer on a deer lease in Bandera, about an hour northwest of San Antonio. I also hunted for pigs and exotics such as axis deer, fallow deer, Dall sheep, and Black Hawaiian sheep. I could also drive down

Didn't do much hunting — no Time

to the Gulf Coast and fish for redfish and trout, or stay closer to home and go bass fishing. In Texas, outdoors options aren't a problem for anyone any time of the year, but finding time to spend in the outdoors was for me.

Yet, when I had the opportunity to partner with Keith, I was all in. The show has proved to be challenging and, as the name suggests, adventurous.

Knowing I would be on television, I had to practice to actually get good at the sport. Consider shooting a bow, for instance. I had been shooting bows, but I also was aware that some of the best bow hunters in the world appeared on outdoor television shows. Fortunately, although I needed to be proficient with a bow, I didn't have to present myself as the greatest bow hunter.

That has been one of the biggest differences between the WWE shows and our outdoors show. Many of the television aspects are similar, but on *MacMillan River Adventures*—unlike wrestling—I don't have to talk a big game to sell tickets. I can be myself as a hunter and be more realistic as I talk about learning to get better. I don't have to be Mr. OutdoorsMania. I'm in a position where I can relate directly to the vast majority of our audience who, like me, love hunting and want to become better hunters. Keith, of course, has been a big help to me and our viewers because of his extensive experience.

I would hate to have to try to count the number of times our cameraman has captured me falling, because I have developed a tendency in the outdoors to clumsily fall into water. Jumping over creeks or swampy areas, I'll trip up on the bank and plummet face-first into the drink.

The last time we filmed in the Yukon, we shot a moose that went down into the river. We tied him to the boat with a rope and were doing our best to pull him down the river when our boat got caught on some rocks. And then the currents got hold of the moose, and we reversed roles, with the moose starting to pull us down the river.

I thought I could save the day by waiting until we were at a place where the river was shallow enough that I could jump in, dig my heels into the rocks, and hold onto the boat so we could regain command of the proceedings. It was a tremendous idea from inside the boat. But where I chose to execute that idea turned out to be bad.

When I thought the river was barely deeper than my boots, I jumped in and dropped until the water was up to my chest. I still was able to dig my heels into the rocks and stop the boat, but when I got back into the boat, I was drenched from head to toe. The temperature was in the thirties, and it took me several hours to completely dry out and warm up.

"I wouldn't have done that," Keith told me when I was back in the boat. "But I'm glad you did it."

———————

Embarrassing moments aside, I've had to earn my stripes in outdoors television. Keith wanted to bring me onto the show because of my name recognition, but sometimes that made things more difficult for the two of us. The other people who host outdoors shows have been wonderful and nice to us, but from the beginning the industry as a whole seemed to go out of its way to let us know that even though I was "big" somewhere else, I wasn't going to receive any free passes in the outdoors world.

I think part of that is because Keith and I have a different way of doing business. We get along really well with people in the industry, but we're not in the clique of outdoor TV guys. A lot of business tends to take place in social settings, and we don't do a lot of just hanging out. We film our shows and then go home to our families. Our hanging out takes place at home with our families, not with others in the industry. For others in the business — and there are some really good folks involved in outdoors — this is their livelihood. I love what I'm doing now, but I don't have to do it as a primary source of income, because I'm still making appearances with WWE.

I hope to reach a point where my outdoors work is my main source of income, because I believe that is the direction in which God is taking me. But if that doesn't turn out to be His plan for me, I know that He will take care of us because in the past He has demonstrated that He will. I don't need to worry about anything.

That's a stance that Keith and I share. The first season our show aired, we had four or five sponsors, and they all knew Keith from previous working relationships. I brought name recognition to the show, but it took a little while before sponsors like Remington and Mossy Oak came aboard. I guess they were waiting to see if I would stick it out. I have stuck to it, and God has definitely blessed Keith and me.

And I'm certainly enjoying His blessings!

When we go to the Yukon, we have to pack our gear on a float plane and fly into the middle of nowhere to land on the river. There are no roads up there, no way in or out except by float plane. The three of us — Keith, our cameraman, and me — stay in a simple wood cabin with rubber-plastic windows. A wood-burning stove is our heat source. The trips last about two weeks, and in our first year there, the weather was so bad that we couldn't have more food brought in. Thank goodness we were able to get a moose down just as we were beginning to run out of decent food. Otherwise, we would have had to get by on candy and granola bars.

We have stayed in great accommodations and in not-so-great places. Regardless of where we are, though, it's always exciting.

I couldn't have said that before my salvation. I was a guy who didn't like being alone, who wasn't able to keep himself company because I didn't like myself. But now I love being alone in a deer blind, fascinated to follow the stars as they fade away, watch the sun rise, and observe nature do its thing undisturbed. The quiet and peaceful environment is the polar opposite of what I became accustomed to during all my years in wrestling, where everything was loud, over the top, and constantly moving. Even the lifestyle of wrestling was fast-paced.

Peace and quiet appeal to me now. I relish having time to sit and be quiet and take in everything around me. That's a big reason why Rebecca and I wanted to move to a ranch. It's hard to describe how much pleasure I gain when, returning from an out-of-town trip, I turn onto the long dirt road that leads to our house. I can almost feel peace filling my lungs. There is just something spectacular about being in the outdoors. I look forward to spending all day on a tractor plowing and planting grazer hay for our deer. I'm still a little shocked when I catch myself thinking that.

When I'm outdoors, I feel close to the Creator. To see the Badlands in the Dakotas and take in their unbelievable rugged beauty and then to go to a mindboggling place like Africa with all its variety is to enjoy His creation. Even at home, as I write this, spring has just kicked in after a winter with more below-freezing temperatures than our typical winter. Everything around our ranch was bare. Then one day I noticed buds appearing. The next day they were starting to bloom. In only a couple of days, everything seemed to suddenly turn from brown to green.

It is amazing to behold, and it's not by accident. I don't see how anyone can spend any time in the outdoors and not believe that there is an Almighty God making all this down here happen.

Faith, family, and outdoors. The passion I now have for the first two came to me later in life than it should have, and I was even late to discover the beauty of the outdoors. But it is fascinating how God molded those three pieces together in my life.

God has given me a purpose in each.

I'm not competing for any Christian of the Year awards. If you ask me how I'm doing, I am liable to say, "Great," "Fantastic," or even "This has been a tough day" if that's what the truth is. But you are not going to hear me answer, "Blessed and highly favored, oh brother!" I don't speak Christianese. That's not who I am. God created all of us different, and I believe He created me as I am for a reason.

Now that I'm a somewhat-experienced outdoorsman, I can tell you that to see a beautiful, white-tailed deer is to know and appreciate that it was created by a loving God. Frogs, on the other hand, are ugly. But the same loving God created frogs for a reason. The frog has its purpose, and so do I.

Maybe I'm a frog. If so, I am okay with that, because I am simply trying to serve my Lord in the area that He has called me to serve, and at this point in time, that is with my family.

In the wrestling business, there was so much talk about legacy. I used to be concerned about what my legacy would be, but I no longer am. Don't misunderstand me, though. I am thankful for my career. I reflect on it and almost get tears in my eyes. I look back at my career in awe, because I was just a kid who wanted to wrestle. I don't want to diminish what happened to me in the ring, because I believe that God gave it to me — even when I was living a life in complete rebellion against Him — so that one day my career would bring glory to Him.

But now my wrestling legacy is irrelevant. The legacy I am working on is the one I am leaving with my children.

Legacy doesn't matter

My goal is very simple: One day, when my body is in even worse shape than it is now, I want my kids to tell me, "Old man, you did us all right. You gave us a good foundation. You taught us right and wrong. You did your best to give us direction."

That's it. I can't dream of hearing my kids tell me more than that.

Cameron must have been six or seven years old when we were in a Bible Study Fellowship class and the teacher asked the adults, "If you asked your kids what the most important thing is in your life, what would they say?"

Of course, I had to ask Cameron for his answer as soon as we had shut the car doors.

He answered with more of a questioning tone when he said, "Wrestling?"

"Really?" I asked incredulously.

"Well," he explained, "it is what you do all the time."

"Oh, man," I said. "I'm so sorry."

That old story came up in a recent conversation with Rebecca, and I had to ask Cameron the question again. He answered without hesitation and with certainty in his voice.

"Us!"

Since my retirement, interviewers have wrapped up their

questions and told me something to the effect of, "You are the only guy we interview who doesn't wrestle anymore that seems to be at peace with his retirement."

I have had people ask me, "You retired just to go home?"

Yes, I did, to help raise my kids.

That itch I have heard retired athletes talk about just isn't there for me. I do not miss the adrenaline rush of being in the ring and hearing the fans either cheer or boo me. It has been that way since 2002, when I became a Christian. My high comes from being home with my family. I'm no longer chasing the dragon—I'm chasing my kids.

That is what God wants for me, and there is no peace better than doing what God has called you to do.

retired to go home

CHAPTER 6
KNOW YOUR IDENTITY

"See what great love the Father has lavished on us,
that we should be called children of God! And
that is what we are!" (1 John 3:1).

In the time I've had to reflect on my career lately, I have been intrigued by how the Lord has brought together elements of wrestling and my faith and even my outdoors adventures.

I can guarantee you that before my first retirement, I could not have imagined writing this: wrestling and Christianity have a lot in common. That awareness is part of the perspective change I have gained as I have continued to grow in my faith and because of the time I've had to think about my career these past four years.

One of wrestling's strengths is veteran wrestlers' willingness to help younger wrestlers develop after they enter the sport. I was fortunate to have Jose Lothario train me and introduce me to wrestling. When I first started wrestling in Mid-South, Ricky Morton and Robert Gibson—The Rock 'n' Roll Express—invited me to ride along with them, and they used our time on the road together to teach me the insides of the sport. Terry Taylor, one of the most passionate people about wrestling I've known, taught me invaluable lessons about how to perform in the ring. Then all along my way up the wrestling ladder, there were others who offered advice or tips that aided my climb.

Older helpful younger

helped forward career

At that time, I just thought of them as good guys who cared enough about their sport to ensure it would remain successful by teaching us young guys how to put on an entertaining show. Now, with my new perspective, I see them as more than that because of how God placed them along my path as part of the plan He had for my life. There was an additional purpose, which I would not discover for years, behind how they were guiding me.

When I retired from the ring, numerous people suggested I should travel around the country speaking about my faith. I have spoken in a few churches, but I chose not to pursue that option so that I wouldn't take time away from home. I understood that people wanted to hear wrestling stories because wrestlers can tell great stories. I got that. But there also was this part of me that was uncomfortable with the idea of being billed as a religious "expert."

The benefit of my not committing to a heavy speaking schedule is that I have had not only more time with my family, but also more quiet time with God. I'm not one of those people who claim to have heard God's voice audibly. I haven't, and don't anticipate that I ever will hear it. But God does put things on my heart. I think He has revealed things to me through the perspective change I have experienced. And I am excited, because writing this book allows me to share some of what I have learned.

I'm still not claiming to be a religious expert, but like Jose, Ricky, Robert, Terry, and the others who helped me, I recognize that I have gained experiences that I can share with those who perhaps are newer to faith than I am. Or who might just listen because they care about wrestling.

As they say, God works in mysterious ways.

My life is proof of that, for sure!

———

Identity is an important concept in both wrestling and Christianity. Every wrestler needs to develop his own identity by which fans will recognize him. Early in my career I tried to distinguish myself from other wrestlers with an outfit that I thought was "out there" and would make people take notice. I wore chaps for a taste of Texas, and the rest of my outfit is best described as Freddie Mercury of the band Queen meets the Village People. It wasn't exactly the manliest concept, but combine my outfit with an authentic attitude of being someone who would do whatever it would take to make it in wrestling, and I thought people would have no choice but to notice that I was different from the others.

HBK outfit

For me to have an unshakeable walk as a Christian, it is vital to know what my identity is—more specifically, that my identity is found in Christ. Even though I have faults, God continually sees me in the image of Christ. God's view of me doesn't change despite what any detractors say about me, and I have to understand that in order to continue the Christian walk He wants me to maintain.

When I went back to wrestling, one of the biggest changes in the business was the focus on wrestlers' identities. *Character* and *character development* were terms we hadn't used during the first part of my career. Before, who we were was just our gimmick. We were wrestlers, and we kept it that simple. But that had changed—now wrestlers also were performers, actors, and entertainers.

I've been credited with having an ability to keep my identity relevant, to continually reinvent myself, so to speak. The funny thing about that is that I never concentrated on what my character was doing or what he would become next.

My character basically evolved as I evolved as a person. I've never considered myself a good actor. I was better at being than acting, so I meshed my real life with my wrestling identity.

I worked hard to learn how to record interviews or monologues in front of the camera—that's known as "cutting promos"—because I cared about having an identity that fans would instantly associate with me, whether in a positive or negative manner. But I didn't stay up at night in my hotel room wondering how my character should feel in particular situations. I am reactionary and emotional, and that came through in my character because I relied on instinct and feelings.

Truth be told, I stumbled onto a lot of good things that hadn't been planned.

Although wrestling is not real, my character did have a lot of real in him. Because of the nature of our sport, fans often struggled to perceive where the line was between the wrestling me and the real-life me. It didn't help them that the line usually blurred. But I believe the real-life aspects I brought into my character were the primary reason I connected with fans.

When I went back to wrestling, WWE had added a writing team. I would chuckle when the new guys asked what roles the creative team had played in well-known wrestling storylines from the past. We didn't have a designated creative team. Vince and Pat Patterson gave us a general direction, and we went out there to cut our TV promos and did whatever we wanted.

Vince, Pat, my opponent, and I were "the creative team" behind my storylines, and we were just throwing things against the wall. What we liked, we kept. What we didn't like, we discarded. That was the extent of it. So I had to adjust to having a writing team around when I returned.

The writers didn't create our matches, but they did script our TV promos. Early on, the head writer came to me and, respectfully, told me that a lot had changed since I had left and that there would be many fans who wouldn't know who I was. He wrote out a bunch of stuff for me to say that would reintroduce me to the audience. I didn't know how to take that. But I was new coming back and had no idea what to expect.

Some of what he wrote was helpful, and I used it. But for the most part, I did what I had always done and went out there on my own little tangent and ventured off to where I instinctively felt led to go. It worked, and I managed to make it work in a way that didn't set off the head writer and his team. I probably would have butchered that in my pre-Christian days.

From that point on, we went through a process to where they would supply me with general bullet points to follow. In turn, I would inform the writers of what I wanted to say and let them write it out in nicer and bigger words so that I wouldn't sound like a dumb hick.

One reason I believe that the second part of my career was better than the first is because of the range and depth of emotions I brought into my job after my comeback. That was a direct result of my faith, which allowed me to tap into real-life emotions like joy, sadness, despair, peace, and conflict over doing right versus wrong, and then bring those into storylines and matches.

A good example is *WrestleMania 24* in 2008, when we brought real life into the storyline for my match against Ric Flair with his career on the line. I was seven years old when Ric made his wrestling debut, and he was an idol of mine growing up.

After it was announced that I would wrestle Ric at *WrestleMania*, I received a call from Kenny Kent, my best friend in high school. Kenny and I had attended wrestling matches together in San Antonio and imitated various wrestlers' moves against each other at home.

"I can't believe it!" Kenny said. "I mean, you are wrestling Ric Flair at *WrestleMania*! When you were fifteen years old and we were watching wrestling on TV, did you ever think you would wrestle Ric Flair?"

I didn't.

A few days before *WrestleMania*, I popped up wide awake at two o'clock in the morning, and my entire match with Ric came to me. I hurried to the dinner table and starting jotting down notes.

Yes, it's pro wrestling—a bunch of men in their underwear fighting each other—but the element of that match that most compelled me was the story of a guy who admired another wrestler and had been inspired by him in the business. I paid attention to all the emotions I felt as I wrote out the match, and after I put the finishing touch on what proved to be one of the greatest endings in wrestling history, teardrops spilled onto the paper.

When we got to Orlando, Florida, for *WrestleMania*, I showed

Emotional Match w/ Flair

my notes to Ric and Michael Hayes. As they looked over the sheet, I observed Ric's eyes moistening. He reached over, patted me on the leg, and said, "Thank you!"

At the end of our match, I sent Ric to the mat with my signature move, the Superkick. I slowly rose to my feet and retreated to the nearest corner. I sized up Ric, still lying in the center of the ring, and started to cue up the fans for my "Sweet Chin Music" finisher. I stomped only once, though, then stopped and looked down to the mat.

Ric struggled to his feet and motioned for me to come toward him. I told Ric, "I'm sorry—I love you," then finished him off with another Superkick. I pinned Ric for the three count, then rolled over next to him on the mat, draped my arm around him, and planted a kiss on his forehead. I quickly exited the ring to leave Ric to have his farewell moment with the adoring fans.

The emotion that night was not acting. I did love Ric. I went from watching him on TV to having him, one of our sport's true legends, accept me as a friend and peer. I can't overstate what he did for our business.

Great match

There was a lot of real life going on in that ring, and it worked. Fans wept all around the stadium. Ric sobbed in the ring and then left to embrace his family in the first row. That match won another Slammy Match of the Year Award. In fact, it has been named by numerous sources as one of the greatest matches of all time. Fans still talk about that ending.

When I had showed Ric and Michael my notes when we set up the match, I'd asked if my idea was okay.

"This isn't a wrestling match," I told them. "This is a love story, for heaven's sake."

I know that sounds very un-wrestling-like. There was no bravado in the plan. Instead, it was filled with humility and vulnerability.

The match reflected a change both in the business and in my personal life.

There was a time when, if we would have attempted that match, we would have been booed out of the building for being wusses. Even

Match Important to HBK

if we had tried to pull that match off then, it would not have played out the same. I couldn't have tapped into those emotions before, because they weren't there. I was selfish then, and selfishness and humility are polar opposites. I pulled off my part of the story because it was easy for me. And it was easy for me because it was real now.

In 2 Corinthians 5:17, Paul writes of Christians, "... if anyone is in Christ, the new creation has come: The old has gone, the new is here!"

I liked the idea of the old me being replaced, but I understood little about what being a "new creation" meant. What it means, I learned, is that when we confess our sins and accept Jesus Christ as our Lord and Savior, we are more than forgiven of our sins. Our lives are also changed. More than that, being a new creation means that we are in the process of being continually changed for the better.

Becoming a Christian doesn't make us perfect. If that were the requirement, I would have been disqualified a long time ago. God changes us, and then with the guidance of the Holy Spirit, we begin the process of learning how to live life a new way, a way that is more pleasing to God than how we had lived.

I had retired because of my back injury in 1998 and returned to WWE in 2002. But I did not make the decision to wrestle full-time again until *WrestleMania 19* in 2003, when I felt certain that God had placed me back in wrestling for a reason.

Vince came up with a storyline for my return in which I would win the World Heavyweight Championship, more as a feel-good story than anything else, and then lose the belt a month later to Hunter. I was fine with the plan, appreciated Vince putting the belt back on me, and went through with it. After losing to Hunter, my next match was against Chris Jericho at *WrestleMania 19*.

All three of those matches went well, with me far exceeding what I expected from myself after the long layoff. The most difficult thing in wrestling is taking time off, whether because of injury or

Faces Chris Jericho

for personal reasons, and then getting back into the ring. Wrestlers understand showing a little bit of rust in the ring when you return, but you still have to perform at a high level. In my first match back, it was as though I hadn't missed a day.

Still new in my salvation, I didn't want to get caught up in everything that goes with being a wrestler again. I was back to headlining pay-per-views, and things were starting to move quickly. I wanted to go home, slow the hamster wheel down a little, and figure out what all was happening. Vince said that he understood, but needed me to cut a promo with Chris. Then I could go home and let him know where I wanted to go from there.

Chris had been in the WCW while I was wrestling, so he and I didn't meet until I came back. We cut our promo, and I made it back to the locker-room area ahead of Chris.

"My God, did you feel that?" Vince exclaimed.

"Feel what?" I asked.

"Out there. You two. Did you feel that?"

"Yeah, it was really good," I said.

"Really good?" Vince shot back. "That is money right there! I can feel it!"

I thought, *Oh my goodness!*

Vince and I hadn't talked about a contract or my going full-time again. I had been doing one-offs so I could take things one match at a time, and Vince had been gracious in allowing me to feel my way around for the time being. I knew that in an enticing way, WWE could be like a merry-go-round that doesn't stop and once you get on, there's no jumping off.

"Look," I told Vince, "I have to take a step back."

"I understand," he said. "But we still want to do this. If you want it, there's something there with you and Jericho."

Chris came back to where we were, all excited like Vince.

"My goodness, did you feel that?" he asked.

I told Chris that I felt it too, but also explained why I needed to get home.

Vince wanted to set up the Jericho — HBK rivalry

"That's fine," he told me. "Just call me when you are ready."

I had about three weeks before needing to be back for *Royal Rumble* and used that time at home for soul searching, praying, and consulting with friends. By the time I had returned for *Rumble*, I felt that a somewhat full-time status was God's plan for me. I told Vince I wouldn't work every weekend house show, but I would do the pay-per-views and TV events one weekend a month.

Vince agreed, and my comeback took a step forward.

return

———

A regular prayer of mine has been, "Lord, open up those doors you want me to walk through and close those you don't want me to walk through." The key part of that prayer is recognizing when it is the Lord who is opening and closing the doors.

There were open doors during my return that I did not step through.

At *WrestleMania 19*, Chris and I were not the main event, but we absolutely tore the house down. That match was when I knew that despite the four years off, I could still deliver in the ring.

WM 19

Although I was not tempted to return to the lifestyle I had led previously in wrestling, the opportunities to resume my old identity were plentiful.

Vince had put the World Heavyweight Championship on me for that one month, and I turned down additional chances to be a world champion again. The champ needed to be on the road all the time and make a lot of appearances. Those were sacrifices I didn't want to make. Being a champion wouldn't have been worth what it would have cost me.

Turned down Champ = Didn't want to travel

The nickname "Mr. WrestleMania" was given to me during my second stint in wrestling. I had already been dubbed The Showstopper and The Main Event in my career. Before, I had allowed those nicknames to become my identity. Now, they were just names. Unlike before, they weren't how I looked at myself outside of wrestling.

I also no longer stormed back through the curtain after a match,

Stopped the post match charge through the curtain

87

as I had earlier in my career, and boastfully challenged the other wrestlers to "Follow that!" The huge chip of pride wasn't on my shoulder anymore.

But a wrestler cannot be humble in cutting a promo. He has to talk with a large show of pride and arrogance. Yet the new me — that new creature — knew I could not be that way in real life. I was so aware of the pride my wrestling character had to show that I often asked God, *Is there going to come a time when You are going to humble me in that respect?* Fortunately, God was much better than fans at separating my character from the real me! I didn't like the thought of having to go through that kind of humbling process. I didn't want the signs that it was time to retire to come through my skill level starting to wane, through no longer being able to deliver good matches, through having my performance deteriorate show by show, performance by performance, pay-per-view by pay-per-view. My desire was to be able to go out in a great match in a *WrestleMania*.

My routine after *WrestleManias* was to spend a couple of minutes alone on my hotel bed before joining my family for celebratory pizza and cookies. I remember a couple of times after a *WrestleMania* when I sat on the bed and wept in awe as I reflected on God's faithfulness.

You have done it for me again, I would tell God.

Without God, I would not have been able to wrestle. Near the end of my career, my body was wrecked. I had no cartilage in either knee. The back was still bad. My left shoulder was in such poor shape that I could barely raise my arm completely above my head. I shouldn't have been able to wrestle at all, much less wrestle well. Yet each time in our sport's biggest spotlight, I would be part of another showstopping match.

Others would tell me I had been amazing in a match, but I knew it wasn't because of me. I knew the ability came solely from the Lord. I don't know if it is possible to be prideful when you consistently acknowledge God's faithfulness in your life.

I've learned that the pride thing only plays well in the ring. It surely doesn't work in the rest of life. When my son was thirteen, he had been making mistakes driving his race car, and I told him to get out of the car after a race.

"Look, if you continue to do that," I told him, "I'm going to have to take you off the track."

"Please don't make me get out of the car," Cameron told me. With tears rolling from his eyes, he told me that racing was what he loved to do. I could see then that he viewed racing the way I had viewed wrestling.

I had to reassess my threat. A year later, he was in a bigger, faster car, and he was racing so much better. He was still making some of the same mistakes, but he had improved from the back of the pack to where he is now in the front of the pack.

That was a case where I couldn't let my pride get in the way and needed to admit that a dad can be wrong.

I still can't give you a great explanation of everything involved in being a "new creation." But I know that God made me one, that He changed my life, and that He gave me a new identity.

Being called The Heartbreak Kid, Mr. WrestleMania, and all those other names doesn't even begin to compare to what it feels like to know that the Almighty God who created the universe calls me His child.

CHAPTER 7
STAY TRUE TO YOUR STANDARDS

"For I am not ashamed of the gospel, because it is the power of God that brings salvation to everyone who believes" (Romans 1:16).

It's easy to declare that you won't compromise your standards. The difficult part is walking that out in your real life.

I experienced that in my return to wrestling as a Christian. That's probably no surprise, given wrestling's image. But the reason why is surprising. Vince and the people at WWE didn't make it hard for me to not compromise my standards. The difficulty came because of fans, members of the wrestling media, and even some peers who wanted to define what my standards should be.

WWE made it easy

To me, being a Christian means knowing that Jesus is my standard-maker and also acknowledging that I will never achieve the standard He set when He lived on earth. Jesus was perfect, and I'm nowhere near it. But that doesn't excuse me from trying my best to live up to His standards.

One of the most reassuring passages in the Bible for me is Romans 8:38–39:

For I am convinced that neither death nor life, neither angels nor demons, neither the present nor the future, nor any powers, neither height nor depth, nor anything else in all creation, will be able to separate us from the love of God that is in Christ Jesus our Lord.

Those two verses comfort me because I'm a screwup. When I became a Christian, I confessed of my sins and God forgave me of all of them. I then entered into a relationship with Him, and my life changed completely. That did not mean that I became sin-free. God loves me. The reason is, simply, because He chooses to. It's not because I have done anything to earn His love.

There is nothing any of us can do to earn God's love. He gives it to us. Romans reassures us that when we enter into a relationship with God, nothing can separate us from that love. When I mess up, I'm confident that God still loves me. When I stumble, I do not unearn His love.

Now, that does not give me free reign to run around being an idiot, as I did while living my old lifestyle. I make every effort I can to live a life pleasing to God. I desire for people who aren't Christians to see the change in my life, to see how that change has lasted, and then want to make the same decision I made to follow Christ. I know, however, that not every single action or thought of mine will be pleasing to God. Jesus lived like that, but He is the only One capable of doing so.

I don't know if God looks down and shakes His head at some of my actions or when my sarcastic sense of humor is on full display. But if I can use that image, when God is looking at what I do and sometimes isn't pleased, I also believe that at the same time He is looking into my heart and recognizes that my aim is to please Him. I'm a hunter, and I don't always hit where I aim. I like to think that God at least takes into account where I'm aiming with my life.

That's why even though I know that I can't live up to the way Jesus lived on earth, He still is my standard bearer. His example is what I'm aiming for. The problems I encountered in not compromising

Me at age ten.

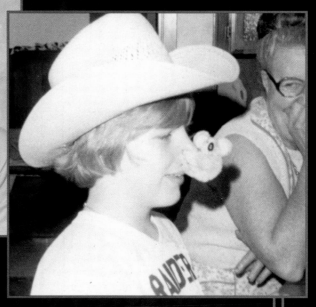

Me entertaining my grandmother
(Nanna); the cowboy hats started early.

Me in my football uniform in seventh grade.

My best friend in high school, Kenny, flipping (suplexing) me into our pool.

Me pressing Kenny into our pool.

Rebecca and me getting married in the Graceland, a wedding chapel in Las Vegas.

The Elvis impersonator who walked
Rebecca down the aisle serenading us;
we weren't exactly classy, but we sure
were crazy about each other.

Me aboard a helicopter in Afghanistan accompanied by our fine men and women of the U.S. military.

Getting ready to get airborne in Afghanistan.

Meeting our military men at a Forward Operating Base (FOB) in Afghanistan as WWE does its yearly "Tribute to the Troops" Show.

Getting off the C-17 in Afghanistan with Triple H in tow.

The family and me at my WWE Hall of Fame induction in 2011.

My daughter, Cheyenne, and me on our annual Father/ Daughter Valentine's Day date night in 2014.

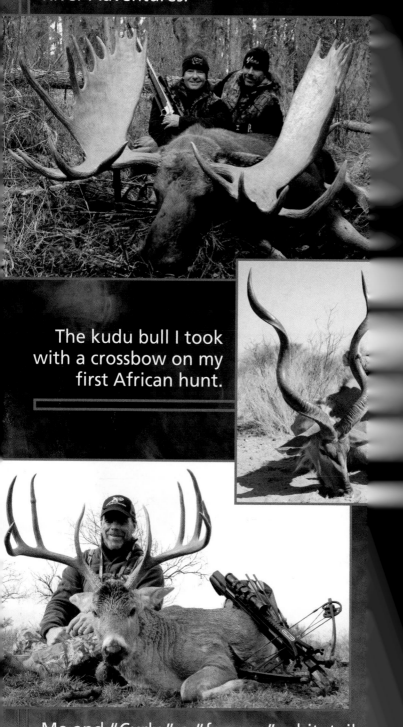

moose filming season 3 of MacMillan River Adventures.

The kudu bull I took with a crossbow on my first African hunt.

Me and "Curly," a "famous" whitetail buck off our ranch in western Texas.

The patented "HBK" pose. After becoming
a Christian, I started incorporating Christian
words and symbols into my wardrobe.

Me superkicking (Sweet Chin Music as it was called) Lance Cade during our match in France, 2008.

Steve Austin and me wrestling at WrestleMania 14.

Triple H and me in our last and much more reserved run as DeGeneration X.

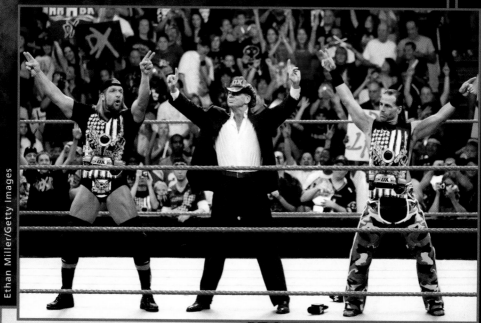

Me and Triple H.

Dropping an elbow from the top rope against The Undertaker.

Me squaring off against The Undertaker in WrestleMania 25 match.

Me standing on the ropes at The Undertaker match.

my standards as a Christian wrestler came from fans and media who believed Jesus' standards were different from what I believed. We were aiming at different spots.

In my return, I wanted to be a good employee while glorifying God. I was on fire for God and wanted to witness on the platform I believed He had brought me back to. I knew I could still be entertaining while being a Christian.

I told Vince there were certain areas in which I would not compromise because of my faith. Vince was receptive to that, saying they would work with me in any way they could and that he couldn't see any reason there would be a problem. Just as changes both in my life and within the company made it possible to bring more emotion into storylines, Vince had been wanting to alter WWE's image so we could attract more family-oriented corporate sponsors. So there was another way in which the timing was right for my return as a Christian.

One big difference from before, I told Vince, would be my involvement in storylines involving women. WWE did not need convincing that sex sells, and sexy women had long played an important role in wrestling. But as a married man, I told Vince I would not be doing anything flirtatious with women. I also told him that I wouldn't be cussing up a storm as I had before. Again, Vince had no problems with that. However, not compromising my standards was harder than I expected.

Many of the challenges I encountered had to do with other people not understanding the world of wrestling. For most, the pretend character that I played on TV was the only "me" that existed. But I wanted to make the real me more visible as a good witness to the fans, which is one reason I wore Christian-themed clothing in the ring. Reaching fans was part of my platform for sure. But there also was this whole other world behind the curtains and the cameras where I had access that few believers did. To me, that was where my witness was most on display. That was where I could make the most positive impact. The guys back there—the other wrestlers, WWE's production people—knew the real me. They had known the previous real me, too.

I knew intimately what that world was like, and it wasn't the same as the circles of influence of those who thought my standards should be more like theirs.

I haven't spent time with Christians called to street ministries, but I can imagine that when they're building relationships with prostitutes and drug addicts, their conversations are vastly different from what is heard in a typical church on Sunday mornings. The standards the street ministers protect are different than mine. And you know what? That's just fine.

It's actually none of my business how they go about their ministries. It is for them and God to determine where they need to draw their lines. God knows the type of people through whom He can reach the down-and-out on the streets. If those ministering believe with all their hearts that God is okay with them reaching people by uttering a couple of words most Christians wouldn't use, then say them, brother!

Hunter and I had been part of the original D-Generation X that helped pioneer WWE's Attitude Era in the 1990s with our crude humor and pranks. The two of us reunited as DX in 2006. Neither of us felt then like doing DX as we had previously, when we were all crude all the time. For one, we were both in our forties, so much of the young punk stuff that was a hit before wouldn't have fit. But then again, DX couldn't exactly come back as choirboys, either. I took on the role of an out-of-the-loop middle-aged man, the nerd to Hunter's hip character. I was the guy with young kids who spent most of his days watching Dora the Explorer, so in character, a lot of Hunter's humor went over my head because I was no longer cool.

Scantily clad women were still part of the DX (and WWE) routine. When they would come out, I would put my hands over my eyes. In our earlier days, women flashing us had been part of our shtick.

crotch chop

Left before Flashing

After we re-formed DX, there was one time when I recall Hunter having a woman flash him. In character, I walked off-camera so I wouldn't be a part of it. Even though that was all acting, I was married and didn't want to give any impression that I would flirt with or be interested in anyone other than Rebecca.

In our original form, DX had been famous for the "crotch chop" and a signature slogan that was really popular with the fans. We would say, "If you're not down with that, we got two words for ya." Then the crowd would shout along with us, "Suck it!" It was all about being funny and obnoxious while doing anything to draw a reaction. When I went back as a Christian, I thought a lot about how to handle that.

In our second time around as DX, I started doing another gesture that took my hands down to my waist, but I didn't do the old crotch chop. With the slogan, we wanted to keep the DX part of our characters as entertaining as possible without my crossing over any lines. What I ultimately decided that I would be comfortable with was for me to be the guy who would say the "If you're not down with that" part to set up Hunter and the crowd for the finisher. Honestly, coming up with that solution wasn't easy. It wasn't a black-and-white issue for me. I knew I would get heat no matter what I did. Ultimately, it came down to following my own convictions, and I was fine with what I chose to do.

There are fans and people in the media who have told me that covering my eyes, walking off-camera, or making a different gesture weren't enough, that I should not have had any association with any of that.

Let's face it, WWE does not have the most edifying programming on television. But I was aware that there would be fans watching us on television — and perhaps some of them would be people the Lord was working on — and they would notice that I was doing something different than my partner.

If that caused them to ask why I was different and a friend could tell them it was because I was a Christian, I would take that in a heartbeat. And if it went undetected on television to most, I knew

Had to say "Damn"

Keith Parker

that the other wrestlers and people behind the scenes were noticing that the changes in my life were real and not for show, not some kind of fad that would soon run its course.

———

The moment when I first grasped my challenge in handling everything that accompanied being a Christian in wrestling came as the result of using the word "damn" in a promo.

I had told Vince that I wouldn't be routinely cursing, but I was asked if I would say "damn" one time as part of a storyline I was working with Hunter. I can't remember exactly what they wanted me to say, but it was something to the effect of "I don't give a damn" that would serve as an exclamation mark to show how angry my character was. My mad act basically was a selling point for an upcoming pay-per-view.

I debated it, decided that I was only acting a part, and said the word.

The backlash was substantial.

Even at my next Bible study back home, Keith Parker pulled me aside when we had finished.

"Brother," he began in the same Alabama drawl with which he had led me in the Sinner's Prayer at my first Bible study. "Can I ask you something?"

"Sure," I answered. Keith and his wife, Priscilla, had become good friends and mentors, and we could talk about any subject.

"How are you doing?" he said.

"Good."

"I watched you Monday night."

"Oh, that's good."

"Well, I noticed that you said a cuss word."

"Yeah," I agreed, and I told him why WWE had asked me to say it for the promo.

We went back and forth for a few minutes, with me explaining that I was just playing a character and that if my appearing so upset with Hunter helped us sell more pay-per-views, saying "damn" once was worth it.

"I just want to say one thing to you," he interrupted. "The devil is a liar."

"I know."

"Well, Shawn, the devil is a liar," he repeated for emphasis.

"I get that," I told him. "Are you saying I shouldn't have said it?"

We debated a little longer before he told me, "You said you weren't going to go back and do any of what you had done before, and you did. And I am just telling you that it's as easy as 1–2–3 and all of a sudden you are back into it."

I got a little upset and tried to explain to Keith that he didn't understand what the wrestling business was like and that it was only entertainment, not real life. I threw out other excuses that I thought were legitimate. I wouldn't admit how uttering "damn" could be the 1 in his 1–2–3 point.

Keith, exemplary spiritual leader that he was, never lost patience with me.

"All right," he concluded. "I just wanted to talk to you about that."

I left in a bit of a huff.

I had been driving all of two miles when I guess the conviction of the Holy Spirit became strong enough that I had to call Keith and apologize.

"I did say I wouldn't do what I had before, and I did," I told him. "I won't do it again."

I am grateful that early in my Christian walk, when I had aimed in the right place but missed the mark, I had a close friend like Keith who was courageous enough to call me out, in love, about damaging my witness.

Promised not to curse

———————

Bringing God into a storyline was another instance when I was reminded of the complications around my stance that I would not compromise my standards.

McMahons
-vs-
Shawn + God

Right after Christmas in 2005, we started an angle between Vince and me leading up to the *Backlash* pay-per-view the following April, when Vince and his son, Shane, would partner in a tag-team match against me and my unique tag-team partner for the night: God.

The feud originated out of the Bret Hart controversy. Shane entered into the storyline, and after I defeated Vince in a No Holds Barred match at *WrestleMania 22*, both of the McMahons confronted me the next night on *Raw* and told me I had defeated Vince only due to an act of God. That set up the *Backlash* match. In one of his promos for *WrestleMania*, Vince even created his own religion, called "McMahonism."

The McMahons were first to the ring for our match, and then Vince took the microphone and introduced God, who was represented by a spotlight that moved toward the ring as harp music played. When the light reached the ring, Vince asked the referee to check "God" to make certain He didn't have any foreign objects on Him. The ref didn't know what to do. That was funny! Then Vince declared it wouldn't matter anyway, because he was making the match No Holds Barred.

The whole intent was to have a handicap match, with me in the ring by myself against the two McMahons. That set up the big ending when, as I was about to defeat the McMahons, the five-man Spirit Squad—interesting name for that match—came to the ring and, with me suddenly outnumbered seven-to-one in a no-disqualification match, cheated so that Vince was able to pin me for the win.

It was fitting that the match took place at *Backlash*, because we received plenty of backlash. Criticism followed two streams. First, that it was a bad idea. Second, that it was offensive.

Match Criticized

Let's start with the first one: It certainly was not a good angle. Okay, I'll go ahead and say it: It was dumb. I had numerous highlights during my career, and that match is not among them. But that was an angle they wanted to do, so we did it.

Now, for those who called the angle offensive and contended I should not have taken part: Up front, let me say that I chose to be a

Shawn took part freely

part of the angle. Neither Vince nor anyone with WWE forced me into it. They brought the idea to me, and I chose to take part.

Vince and I had several discussions about the angle before it started, and we kept talking about it as the storyline progressed. All throughout, he sought my input. He kept asking if I was okay with the storyline.

"Obviously, we don't want to offend anyone," he stated early on.

"Obviously, we are going to offend people," I told him. After all, we were WWE, and offending people generally went with the territory.

"I just don't want to cross the line," Vince said. "Let me know if anything will be in bad taste."

I assured Vince that I would not go along with the angle if I didn't feel comfortable with it. I also said that I didn't feel like he was mocking my faith. I did tell him, however, that he was mocking the church. More accurately, his character was mocking the church.

I gave Vince my analysis: "You are playing the part of people who mock faith every day by the way they live their lives. They disrespect the church, disrespect themselves, and disrespect a lot of stuff. To me, what you're doing is symbolism. I get it."

In my opinion, Vince's character was so far over the top in what he was saying that it was obvious it wasn't real. I thought he was hilarious. But then again, as that storyline demonstrated, it can be difficult for wrestling fans to separate what is real from what isn't.

Perhaps, without realizing it, I had factored in what I knew of the *real* Vince. Vince is a great guy who is nothing like the way he portrays himself on television. He's a hard-working son-of-a-gun who is the epitome of trying to be the macho guy who has an answer for everything. Inside, though, he is a decent, feeling guy. Vince makes me laugh just by the personality he has. He is a wealthy guy who at the same time is also a dipstick, which I guess is what appeals to me about him. He smartly runs a gigantic corporation, yet still enjoys having silly fun.

When my lifestyle was out of control, Vince never gave up on me. I've heard it said that because of my wrestling ability, it was in Vince's best interest to keep me around regardless of how much trouble I caused. Yes, I was a commodity of his. Yes, there were others he had good reason to keep around for his company's bottom line, but instead he let them go. For whatever reason, he never did that to me.

Then when I returned as a Christian, he was nothing but accommodating. I told Vince about the apostle Paul and how he had been a bad guy named Saul who persecuted Christians before his life was turned around on the road to Damascus and then ended up writing a majority of the New Testament.

"You could do stuff like that," I told Vince. "This empire you have created here—who knows the kind of good you could do from this place?"

"Oh, please!" he replied. "I wouldn't go that far."

At least I was able to plant a seed.

Vince may have resembled Saul more than Paul, but he was not the evil guy he was portraying in the God angle.

And Vince was my boss. Even though I wasn't a fan of the overall angle—despite Vince being funny in his role—I was attempting to be a good employee without compromising my standards.

I once heard Ted DiBiase make a comparison that fits my take on participating in the God angle. Ted, a solid Christian and effective minister, got into wrestling about a decade before me. Ted wrestled as "The Million Dollar Man" and mostly as a heel. I heard Ted speak at an Athletes International conference a few years ago, and a kid asked Ted how he could have been a bad guy and a Christian at the same time.

Ted told the crowd that what he did as a wrestler was the same as someone playing Satan in a church play. That actor could play the role of Satan and still be a Christian. Ted's analogy hit home with me. I doubt there is anyone who would walk up to the dude playing Satan and ask, "How's your walk going, brother? Are you stumbling? I noticed last week that you were laughing when Jesus was crucified."

Playing Satan in the church play doesn't make the guy any less of a Christian than the actor portraying Jesus.

I did not want to do anything in wrestling that would negatively impact my witness. I had some say in what I would do as part of my job, and I made those decisions as they came up. But I also had to consider my witness behind the curtains with the guys who knew me best and were watching me. I could have hurt my witness with them by raising a huge stink about WWE wanting to bring DX back or whatever the issue at hand was.

As for the controversial God angle: I thought it was a dumb idea, but I was at least excited that God was included in a WWE storyline. I mean, Vince McMahon was letting me talk about God on his show! I spoke with some people who saw it that way, who said it was "huge" that we were sharing God with a large audience. More people, though, didn't see it that way. They were so distracted by the words of Vince's character—and I go back to the symbolism of what we see in real life with people mocking the church—that they lost sight of the fact that in the crazy world of WWE I was able to represent God and glorify Him in front of millions of people.

As I said earlier, I prayed many times for God to open the doors I needed to go through and close the ones I didn't need to go through. Throughout the criticisms I had to remain more concerned about doing what God wanted me to do in step with His plan for me in wrestling than about what others thought I should be doing.

I learned an important lesson about knowing whom to please first and foremost.

CHAPTER 8
AIMING TO PLEASE

"Am I now trying to win the approval of human beings,
or of God? Or am I trying to please people? If I were
still trying to please people, I would not be a
servant of Christ" (Galatians 1:10).

———————

Paul told the believers in the church at Colossae that he and Timothy prayed that the Colossians would live a life that pleases God.[3] I like the thought that simple ol' me can please the Creator of the universe. That's mind-boggling.

It also is amazing to consider that it seems like it is easier sometimes to please the Almighty God than it is to please other people like me.

I have spent thirty years in a business centered on fiction. I don't say that wrestling is fake. We pounded the daylights out of each other. Believe me, the pain and injuries were real. But wrestling is make-believe, with Vince deciding whether you get to be a champion or not. Wins and losses are not real.

The wrestling business, however, also is what the fans want it to be. Some were fine with it and just loved the drama and the stories. But for some fans the feuds we had going on in the ring were as real as the person sitting next to them at the match. What made it tough

———————

3   See Colossians 1:3–14.

for us as wrestlers was that we could never know which it was going to be on any given day to any given person.

I had friends at church who said they understood that wrestling was entertainment but still asked how I could have Superkicked Hulk Hogan. Well, it was a pretend match, and we decided beforehand that when he raised his hand and looked away, I would kick him. Me "kicking" Hogan was a real issue for them.

Daniel Bryan is a good young wrestler whom I trained. We once worked an angle where I was a special guest referee, and when Daniel attacked Hunter, I introduced Daniel to some Sweet Chin Music— my signature Superkick. I got called a sellout and backstabber for kicking someone I had helped bring into the sport.

It was pretend!

The predicament all of that created for me as I tried to keep my Christian walk in the sport was that there was no way I could win with everybody. I just couldn't please all the fans.

No matter what I did, there would be some who thought I shouldn't have done it, or should have done it a different way.

Frankly, after I returned to wrestling as a Christian, I caught more flak from Christians than I did from wrestling fans who weren't believers.

I learned quickly to aim to please God and leave the rest up to Him and the people to work out how they should feel about me. I realize that sounds harsh, but I had to take that approach after discovering that it was possible to do what I believed would please God, yet that would still not be good enough to please some Christians.

It wasn't just in wrestling where I experienced this.

Keith Mark warned me before our first outdoors show aired that I would catch heat for hunting. I admit to getting caught off guard about that. I had been raised in Texas, and even though I didn't hunt growing up, it never occurred to me that people could get uptight over another person hunting. I learned.

I was shocked by the number of people who thought they were

Hunting — Bible not against it

quoting Bible verses to support their opinions that I shouldn't hunt animals. Look, I've read the Book multiple times, and it doesn't say that.

Wrestling fans can easily be susceptible to becoming bitter and resentful because we do overdramatize in our sport. Our job is to hard-sell storylines. The fallout is that there are fans who lose a grasp of reality and will never admit it!

What we do for three hours on a Monday night show has nothing to do with real life. And while we determine the message, we cannot control how it is received.

a show — Fake!

When I played the role of a heel, my job was to stir up emotions to the point that fans hated my character. It was only natural that some of those emotions were going to spill over toward the real me. I understood that.

I don't want this to come across as complaining. It was part of the job for all of us. We knew it was coming, and we dealt with it.

Instead, I want to communicate what it's like in the wrestling business, because there was a time when I worried about what people thought about me. Even though I said publicly that I didn't, I did worry about it. Opinions were so varied that if I got caught up in trying to please both sides, I would only wind up placing myself in the middle of a giant tug-of-war.

One of the many things I love about being a Christian is that I can put my focus on pleasing God above all others. I still seek affirmation, but now it is from God. I want people to like me — the real me — but I know from experience that is not possible in every case.

There is no shortage of people willing to give me advice on what I should and shouldn't do, or how I should do things. As a Christian, I had to get comfortable in my own skin and in my relationship with God so that I wouldn't wind up in the middle of that tug-of-war and become distracted or bogged down in areas that aren't healthy for me.

I know there are people who contend I am the greatest wrestler who ever lived. It could be easy to get caught up in that type of praise. But you know what? I don't believe that God really cares if I was the greatest wrestler ever. I believe that He cares instead that after I became a Christian, I used my gift for His glory.

It is at best debatable whether I'm the best wrestler of all time. But the likelihood is that there will be another wrestler, or multiple wrestlers, who will come along and be so good in our sport that my name is removed from consideration. Will the people's views of me change then? You bet they will. But God's view of me won't.

When the time comes, I will stand before God to give an account of my life, and I don't anticipate God asking whether I was a better wrestler than Ric Flair.

After becoming a believer, I discovered Christian music. I didn't even know such a genre existed. I've always been a country music guy at heart, but I got hooked on the songs of three bands in particular: Casting Crowns, MercyMe, and Third Day. Those three have really ministered to me with their music. One of my favorite songs is Casting Crowns' "Lifesong," which speaks to our lives being a song through which we can bring a smile to God.

I think about that song a lot, because on that day when I give an account of my life, I believe that God is going to look at my life as a whole, and He is the Judge I need to please. There are plenty of people around who like to judge me. (And you probably have judges in your life too.) Because of my chosen profession, I've had to develop thick skin. This goes back to knowing my identity in Christ and being comfortable with who I am now, so those have become non-battles for me.

Admittedly, there is a part of me that wants to tell someone who thinks I'm a horrible Christian, "Well, the day I stand before you and … oh, never mind. I am never going to stand before you, am I?" I might think that sometimes, but I don't say it. It has become easier for me to discard that type of unfounded criticism.

In Acts 1:8, Jesus told His apostles that they were to be His witnesses "in Jerusalem, and in all Judea and Samaria, and to the ends of the earth."

I have been asked how I could be a Christian and work in wrestling. I answer by saying, "Jesus said to take the gospel everywhere. He didn't say to take it everywhere but the WWE. Just like He didn't say to take it everywhere except the slums."

Jesus said to be His witness everywhere, and I do what I can where I am.

Some have contended that I could be doing even more and suggested I start a speaking ministry.

"If I feel like He calls me to do that, I will," I respond. "But I haven't felt called to go there."

God meets us where we are and can use us where we are if we allow Him to. I've been amazed at how God has been able to use me, so I've learned not to put limits on the ways in which He works. As a result, I don't go around telling other people how they should minister, because none of us knows what God is telling anyone to do or what His overall plan is; we can usually see only our little piece of it. *Not Preachie*

I laugh thinking about Jonah not wanting to go minister in Nineveh. After he spent three days and nights in the belly of a giant fish, Jonah's surroundings helped him decide that Nineveh might not be such a poor destination after all. Still, after ministering in Nineveh, Jonah complained to God because he didn't like the way He was doing things.

God's answer to Jonah, in the words of the Shawn Living Translation: "You don't know what I am doing here, so shut your piehole and get to work."

That is what I try to do. Some may not agree with how I do things, but as long as I pray and spend time reading God's Word and sense that I am doing what He wants me to do where He wants me to do it, then I figure that I am pleasing God, and that is the best that I can do.

―――――

There is one part of pleasing people that has been a struggle for me since becoming a Christian. When I went back to wrestling, I wanted to be a good witness and a shining light. Fully aware that I was representing the Lord in everything I did, I was very conscious of how I presented myself.

Perhaps the area I struggled most with that concerned autograph seekers.

As a non-Christian, I was accommodating with fans when I wanted to be and not accommodating when I didn't want to be. If I upset someone by not signing an autograph, I didn't care. There was no conviction whatsoever if I said no.

But when I went back full-time as a Christian, I struggled with how accommodating I should be. I've read the story about Jesus being surrounded by a crowd and sensing the woman touching the hem of His garment.[4] The story says that it was so crowded that the people were pressing against Jesus. There were other accounts in the New Testament, too, of Jesus being in a crowd because everybody knew who He was, and He never lost it with the people. There were times when He would go off on His own, or with the disciples, to get away and rest, but I never read of a case where Jesus lost it in front of everybody.

That became a little burdensome. I began to question whether I was allowed to say no, whether I could turn down anyone. If I wasn't making everybody happy all the time, was I being a bad Christian?

Consider the mornings after a *Raw* when, on three or four hours of sleep, I would wake up at five o'clock, go to the airport, and have people asking for my autograph as I was trying to make it through the security line. There were times I politely said no, but then I'd clear security and wonder whether I had been a bad witness.

I am very protective of my family when we are out together. I feel for my kids, because they have had to share me with others every day of their lives. I get recognized pretty much every time I leave the house, and my kids have never had 100 percent of my attention when we are together in public.

One day we were walking through a mall when a man asked for my autograph. I declined, but he pressed for me to sign anyway.

---

4   See Luke 8:40–48.

"Come on, man!" he insisted.

"No," I told him. "I am with my family."

He walked away, and I began to feel horrible. Trust me, before becoming a Christian, I would not have given the man a second thought. But as a Christian, I began to wonder if I had done wrong by not signing.

We looked for the man in the mall. We found him, and I apologized and signed for him.

We have made several family trips to Disney World, and when we go there, it is completely family time. Fans will request an autograph or ask to pose for a picture with me. I explain that I am on a family trip and that I hope they can understand why I am not signing or posing with anyone that day.

Most of the time the fans do seem to understand. Once in a blue moon, though, I encounter people who want what they want and that's it, with no regard for my family time. But even with the people who understand, I know I have disappointed them. I used to be concerned that they would go back home and tell friends that I was a jerk and wouldn't sign for them. Or that I'm not really a Christian because I said no.

Now I just hope a friend of theirs will hear their story and say something like, "He was at Disney with his family, and you are calling him a jerk because he wouldn't sign an autograph when you interrupted his family time?" Then perhaps that person will understand that I had a legitimate reason for not signing that day.

When I am not with my family, I try to be as accommodating as possible. I have picked up, however, the difference between a fan who wants an autograph for himself and someone who wants an autograph (or, usually, autographs) to sell online. I've encountered people outside my hotel at three o'clock in the morning, holding a two-year-old kid and saying they want autographs for the kid. That child has no idea what's going on.

"Take him home and put him to bed, please," I've told them, "because I am going to bed."

Then there are situations when I need to say no. No celebrity has said yes to everything. It can't be done. There are times when I can't be accommodating because of my schedule or whatever. Those are the times that gnaw at me because I know that what can seem to me like an insignificant autograph actually is meaningful to others.

As I read the Gospels, I never saw a time when Jesus was a doormat. Jesus found a perfect balance, and for me it has been an ongoing search to find the line to walk between making people happy and giving up too much in order to do so.

That's why I never present day-to-day Christian living as a cakewalk. It isn't always easy. There are situations we face for which we can't go find a verse in the Bible that gives us the specific answer, but the Bible does give us principles we can apply to any situation we face.

For me, that means living a life that is pleasing to God. I know I make mistakes, and I know I let people down. When I feel convicted, I try to find that person and make amends. But then again, I know that it is impossible to please everyone.

We can only see each other's actions. That's all we have to go by. I'm thankful that God sees more than our actions. He sees our hearts. And if we can please God, I figure we're doing all right.

Chapter 9
Self-Discipline
Brings Rewards

*"… let us throw off everything that hinders and the sin
that so easily entangles. And let us run with perseverance
the race marked out for us" (Hebrews 12:1).*

Tony Falk might have been the last person in wrestling in a position to advise me about the importance of working out.

Tony, who made a career out of wrestling on undercards (preliminary matches before main events), was one funny dude. For a while he dressed like British singer Boy George and wrestled as "Boy Tony." At another point in his career—inspired, I guess, by Tupac Shakur—he went with a rapper getup and billed himself as "2 Falk 4 Sure."

"This is going to be a body business," Tony told me a few months after I had started my career with Mid-South. Wrestling, he staunchly preached, would soon belong to those who worked out.

Tony proved prophetic—except that he did not follow his own advice.

Tony was never in shape. To his credit, he also told me that working out regularly would be the most difficult work I would ever do in wrestling. Tony must have spoken from knowing his own weakness, even though he constantly told me he was getting ready to start working out. I saw Tony a couple of years after I had left Mid-South.

Working out
discipline

He was still overweight and still proclaiming he was about to start going to the gym.

Good ol' Tony.

I'm glad I listened to him. Working out proved beneficial for my character and for me as a performer, because I soon noticed that the better shape I was in, the better matches I could put on.

One thing I prided myself on was being able to wrestle long matches and still be strong at the end. In 1989, when I teamed with Marty Jannetty as The Midnight Rockers, we put on a string of Marathon matches against Jacques and Raymond Rougeau. Marathon matches were an hour in length, and the team with the most "wins" during the match was declared the winner. Going an hour in a match was a big deal, and we did a series of them in house shows. That earned Marty and me some stripes early on.

I wasn't a gym rat. I didn't enjoy working out. I worked out because I had to. I would work out at least thirty minutes a day, but I wasn't going more than an hour. That was my max.

I remember an eight-hour flight we took to Europe. We flew all night and landed in the morning. The natural inclination was to take the morning off and go straight to the hotel bed because we had a show that night. Instead, even though I didn't want to, I decided to push myself and hit the gym.

That story comes to mind because I turned out to have a great workout. Some of the best workouts I've had—when you're pushing yourself, breaking a big sweat, and feeling the sense of accomplishment that comes when you know you've pushed your body to the limit—occurred when I didn't want to go to the gym. My body would be saying "not today." I was tired, and I wanted to stay in bed and blow off the workout and make up for it the next day. But then something within me would remind me that working out was best for me.

Resistance builds strength—all resistance, in one form or another. We don't like resistance because it is difficult, but overcoming resistance is what makes us stronger because that is how muscles are built.

I still work out in the mornings, although not with the intensity of my wrestling days. I do yoga and functional movements. I also borrow from CrossFit and do exercises like burpees, pushups, and chin-ups. I don't do much with weights these days, choosing body-weight and low-impact exercises to make working out easier on my knees, back, shoulder, and joints. I'm geared now toward quality of life workouts, and I am in decent shape for a man approaching fifty who doesn't need to be in great physical condition anymore professionally.

The benefits of what I didn't want to do became a routine for me that goes on to this day.

Stays in shape but not hardcore

I had numerous people like Tony Falk, in my early days as a Christian, encouraging me to spend time each day studying God's Word and in prayer.

When I first became a Christian, waking up and reading the Bible was easy. After all, I was on fire for God! There came a time, though, when it wasn't effortless, and the easier action would have been to stay in bed a little longer and catch up on my reading the next day. But something would stir up within me that would cause my body to overrule my thoughts and make the effort to get out of bed and read. Like with the workout after the long flight to Europe, there have been many times when the extra effort proved worthwhile and God spoke to me in special ways on days when I read more out of need-to than want-to.

As an example, I think back to the period when the building was for sale, I was leaving wrestling, and our family was moving from San Antonio again. There were mornings when I woke up discouraged because I felt that I had been obedient and thought that there-fore things should have been going better than they were. At times, I wanted to throw my hands up and say, "Forget it." But then I would open the Bible or a devotional book and have my spirits lifted by a topic that wasn't remotely close to what I was dealing with. There is something about God's Word being filled with hope that it gives you

enough to soldier on through the day. Reading the Bible and devo-
tionals reminds me that everything is going to be all right.

Whenever I feel like everything and anything is going to hell in
a handbasket, I read Job. That book causes me to think, *My children
are healthy and they're here. They wake up in the morning, they have ten
fingers and ten toes, and they're walking upright. Life ain't all bad.*

Nothing puts life in perspective for me like Job. I mean, he lost
his family, and that really strikes me as the ultimate blow to have to
endure. I marvel that Job didn't curse God. I've never cursed God as
in, *I'm done with You.* But I have certainly told Him what's on my
mind. So I'm always amazed that Job continued to push through his
tough times. He's pretty darned impressive.

Rebecca and I have a routine when I'm home. We wake up and
I put a heating pad on my back to loosen the cranky thing up. Then
we go to the kitchen, where we talk while she drinks her morning
coffee and I start my day with an energy drink. Rebecca then studies
from her Bible while I do my morning reading. We talk some more,
including sharing what we have just read. Then I'm off for my morning workout and stretching while the kids get up and get ready for
homeschool.

That's our morning routine, but I will tell you that I have not
read the Bible every single day since I became a Christian. That's
important for me to share because I know that it is easy for Christians
to beat themselves up if they fall one day behind in their read-the-
Bible-in-a-year program or whatever spiritual discipline they follow.

Like probably every Christian, I have gone through my dry spells
when I haven't studied the Bible for a few days. The main encouragement I have for others who encounter dry spells is to know that you
are not alone, it does not mean you're a failure as a Christian, and it
certainly does not mean that since you can't have a perfect record,
there is no reason to try. Those dry spells have served to help me
realize the benefit of spending time in God's Word. I don't feel as
complete when I fail to read the Bible or a good devotional in the

(handwritten margin note: Morning Routine)

morning. When I start the day with Scripture, it just somehow makes the day go better, like I've checked in with God to start my day.

When we take our *MacMillan River Adventures* show on the road, I sometimes have to get out of bed at insane hours. I barely wake up on time as it is, and I can't imagine getting up thirty minutes earlier to read the Bible. And when I'm sitting out in a deer blind in the middle of who knows where, I surely know that when the hunt is over, I'm going straight to taking a nap instead of reading.

Although I've missed days of Bible study, there has not been one day since I got saved that I have not spent time in some type of communication with God. Even during my dry periods, I have intentionally kept the line of communication there.

I can be in the Yukon, driving up and down a river looking for a big old moose, and think about how I never would have imagined I would be in that place. I will think about that opportunity, then how I have a beautiful wife and two wonderful children back home who love me and miss me, and I just have to say, "Thank You, Lord."

I consider that a form of prayer. I don't know how it is possible to *not* do that every day.

Paul wrote in 1 Thessalonians 5:17 that we should "pray continually." A few translations say "pray without ceasing." That threw me in my early days as a Christian. I read that and thought, *'Without ceasing'? You can't do that. Are you kidding me?* (Except on airplanes. They make me nervous. I have no trouble praying without ceasing when I'm on a plane.)

It was a major relief when someone explained to me that what Paul means there is not that we should always be praying actual words to God. We couldn't do that. Instead, Paul was instructing us to pray regularly and to always be mindful of God's presence in our lives.

I can do that, I thought.

After I went back to WWE, the only time I had to stand firm against one of Vince's requests was to keep my schedule where

Rebecca and I could make our weekly Bible studies. Our studies were that important to both of us.

Rebecca took part in a Bible study during the day on Tuesdays and I had one on Tuesday nights. With our kids homeschooled, I needed to be home Tuesdays to be with them while Rebecca went to her group.

I had been appearing on Monday night *Raw*, and The Undertaker had been on Tuesday night's *SmackDown* episodes seemingly forever.

Vince / no agents

Vince didn't like to work with agents, and I never had an agent to negotiate my contracts. Vince and I handled things face-to-face, and when we were talking about a contract for me, he brought up the idea of my moving to *SmackDown*. I told him I wouldn't do that. He asked why, and I told him I had to be home Tuesday mornings so my wife could go to her Bible study, and then my Bible study was on Tuesday nights while *SmackDown* was being shot.

Turned down money for bible study

Vince told me matter-of-factly that not moving to *SmackDown* could cost me in my contract. He suggested that instead of offering me $1 million, he would offer me $500,000. I know that was a lot of money either way, so I'm not asking for any sympathy! The significance for me, though, was that with the loan we had taken out to purchase the land and construct the building, looking at the possibility of having my income cut in half really got my attention. If for some unexpected reason our loan would have gotten called in, I probably would have had to go through all my savings to pay off the loan. Then what would happen?

That was a major decision for me—probably the biggest financial test I had encountered. To that point in my life, I had been able to earn my financial security through working as a wrestler. But now, confident that God wanted me to wrestle less so I could be with my family more, I would have to trust God and rely on Him to ensure that my family would be provided for financially.

I told Vince that I wouldn't move to Tuesday nights and that I didn't care if it meant making half the money. Vince wasn't trying to be a difficult negotiator—he was honest, sincere, and upfront, and I was the same with him. I understood what he was thinking, too, from an employer's standpoint. If an employee tells his boss that he wants to work twenty hours a week instead of forty, obviously his paycheck will be affected. The fact is, our family received more out of Rebecca's and my Bible studies than anything money could buy us. Those Bible studies were an important part of our lives, and we weren't going to give those up. Vince and the company were always very supportive of me in that respect.

In the end, Vince decided it was best to keep me on *Raw* and keep Taker on *SmackDown* without me, but I was not going to move to Tuesday nights no matter how much it would have cost me in my contract.

Pastor Hagee used to say from the pulpit, "You can't take your next breath without Almighty God allowing it." That's one of those things that I heard enough, and I began to realize, "You know, he is really right about that. Once again, here is another day the Lord has given me and all this around me."

One of the greatest things my salvation has given me is the ability to live in a state of thankfulness. I don't have the ability to *not* acknowledge God on a daily basis.

It has never been difficult for me to be thankful. I was a good kid, raised by parents who worked their tails off. But none of that mattered, because when I went out on my own, I screwed it up. That fall from grace means I grasp what I am worthy of—which is not much, if anything—and when I compare that to what I have, what I've had, and everything that I've lived through, how could I not be thankful?

Thankfulness is an important word for me. I shake my head as I look around and see the sense of entitlement that has become prevalent in society today. Before becoming a Christian, I felt entitled to be treated a certain way or to be given certain things because of my accomplishments. Becoming a Christian provided me with a different

Entitled

view of my achievements. I'm still proud of them. I did work hard so that good things could happen to me. But now, instead of feeling entitled because of my accomplishments, I feel thankful that God gave me the ability to achieve them. My accomplishments aren't for me; they are a way to bring glory to God. I don't waste my time answering the question of whether I was the greatest wrestler. Thank you for considering me, but that question is totally subjective. And, more important, who cares?

Don't care

If you want me to talk about an accomplishment I am truly thankful to have had, let me tell you about holding my son and daughter right after they were born. Now I can look at the pictures from when they were younger and notice how much they have changed. They have grown from being little babies to, in some regards, little adults. Cameron is taller than I am now. He knows I'm a pinhead, but he loves me anyway. Cheyenne is a precious young lady. At this point in their lives, they are good, quality human beings. That is phenomenal.

Kids

They have a mother who has poured herself into their lives. And even though there were some things I screwed up, through God's grace and mercy I am blessed to be a real part of their lives. In the mornings I come back from my workout, and they say, "Good morning, Daddy," and I get to hug them. We're healthy, we're together, we love each other, and we all get along. How could I not just sit in awe of that and be thankful for what God has given me?

Thankful Kids + Family

Chapter 10
"Be the Man"

"Have I not commanded you? Be strong and courageous.
Do not be afraid; do not be discouraged, for the LORD
your God will be with you wherever you go" (Joshua 1:9).

Ric

My buddy Ric Flair was widely imitated for his catchphrase, "To be the man, you gotta beat the man!" I had my runs in WWE as "the man," but not until I grew as a Christian did I understand what it means to be a *real* man.

If I were ever to meet James Dobson or Chuck Swindoll, I don't know if I would hug them or punch them! I feel that I've read every book on being a father and manhood, and the books those two have written have reshaped my definition of what it means to be a man. If I were to punch either one, I promise it would be a punch shared out of love. In fact, I'd be embarrassed to say how much they have made this old wrestler cry.

Professional success used to define manhood for me, and my definition included a distinctly physical element. The defining characteristic of a man was that he was *tough*. And I was tough. 98

I crushed my back in the Casket match against The Undertaker. I broke three ribs five minutes into a match with Ric and completed the match. I wrestled with a blown out anterior cruciate ligament and torn medial meniscus in a knee. I hurt my knee during a match

Injuries

in Europe and wrestled in tag-team matches to finish the tour. Then when we returned to the United States, I aggravated the injury in a bout, and the following night, after getting around behind the curtain on crutches, I wrestled because fans had voted me into a spot in a pay-per-view match. Only after that match did I take time off for the surgery I badly needed. That's just a sampling of the injuries I wrestled through.

I had doctors tell me I would never wrestle again, but I did. I had doctors watch me perform in person and tell me there was no physical way I should have been able to do in the ring what I had just done. I wore my toughness like a badge of honor. But now, looking back, that physical toughness means very little to me. Actually, it sometimes strikes me as pretty dumb. All I did was hurt myself worse.

Some of those matches I listed took place after I became a Christian. Early in my Christianity, the physical pain that Jesus Christ endured on the cross appealed to me as a man. I wrestled with parts of me broken and ripped and torn apart, and I could wrestle hurt like nobody's business. So when I considered the pain that Christ endured, I could connect with that, but on a much smaller scale, of course. Jesus was *tough*!

As I've matured as a Christian, there has been a shift in how I connect with Jesus. He's still physically tough in my book, but now I am more fascinated by His mental and emotional toughness.

At first, I didn't want to disappoint Jesus because He had died for my sins. I'm still moved by the compassion of Christ in giving His life to make my salvation possible. But now I have added this connection with Him through the fact that when He hung on the cross, He bore not just my sins, but the sins of all the people who hurt Him. I cannot comprehend how immeasurably mentally, emotionally, and physically tough Jesus had to be to do that.

Since I've left the unicorns-and-rainbows stage of my faith, I've had people hurt me, including people who were close to me. You know by now that I don't mind telling it like it is, and I don't mind telling you that when I got hurt, there were moments when my instinct was to think, *Phooey on them. They did it; they deserve that.* I've wanted to rip my hair out and knock somebody out. I've been hurt that badly, and that makes me more impressed by how Jesus handled His emotions, because I've been hurt only a fraction of how much the people around Jesus hurt Him. He was betrayed by one of His chosen disciples, and the others didn't exactly prove to be the strongest support group. And those were the people who were closest to Him.

When I try to imagine what it would be like to multiply what I've experienced with people hurting me and then still be able to display the compassion and the forgiveness that Jesus did, I can only conclude that when Jesus walked this earth, He was one tough man. Physically, mentally, *and* emotionally.

We throw the words *forgiveness* and *grace* around so much that I am concerned they could lose their meaning, as has happened with the words *love* and *great*. If you examine forgiveness and grace in the life of Jesus, it becomes clear that it takes a man of vast integrity and character.

Unfortunately, that is the type of man our society has come to mock. That man doesn't come across as cool according to the world's standards. Society likes to change its perception of what is cool and what isn't. What's cool today wasn't cool a few years ago, and it won't be cool a few years from now. I experienced that in my wrestling career. Back in the 1990s, everybody thought my character was incredibly cool. In the next decade, it was still considered okay, but it wasn't as cool as it had been in the '90s. My character hadn't changed, but society's perspective on what's nifty and cool had.

As Christian men, we can't be swayed by society's changing perspectives. If we do, we will have to change our beliefs to keep up with what's currently perceived as correct. But even that will change, too, with time. The Bible hasn't changed and will not change. God's Word is for all time, and I'm much more interested in God, not society, thinking I am cool.

I desire to be a man with integrity and character, because those are the traits of a *real* man.

The biggest challenge men face is to be the kind of man who operates in contrast to the world's definition of *man*. There is intense conflict between the two, and what our society desperately needs is for more men to step up and become warriors of strength and grace.

I have a warrior mentality, and one of my favorite Old Testament warriors is Joshua.

When I returned to WWE from retirement, I was made a member of the New World Order (nWo) stable of wrestlers, joining Kevin Nash, Sean Waltman (X-Pac), Big Show, and Booker T. But there were no plans for me to wrestle. Then Kevin got hurt during a match, and I came up with a storyline in which I would take up for my friend and challenge Vince to a Street Fight. Vince had abused Kevin to the point that he got hurt, the angle would go, just as Vince had pushed me to where I had gotten hurt and had to retire.

It would be a one-match-only storyline, and when I called and pitched the idea to Vince, he said he would get back with me.

That's when I began wondering if I was doing the right thing. There had been no mention of me wrestling again until I suggested it to Vince.

I had just reached the book of Joshua in my Bible-reading schedule. Moses had died, and Joshua was taking over leadership of the people of Israel. Joshua was a dude I easily connected with because he had been Moses' right-hand man, an underling who was promoted to lead the entire nation.

The secondary role was one I knew well. Although I often had worked as the main guy in the groups I wrestled with, in real life I wasn't the leader. When I was part of the Rockers tag-team with Marty, I followed his lead because he was a little older than I was and because I thought he had more of a business mind. When Kevin came to WWF as my bodyguard, he was older and wiser than I was, so he led the way. With DX, Hunter was younger, but he was a little more centered than I was.

With my lack of experience being out front, I could sense how intimidating Joshua's assignment might have seemed to him. Three times in the first half of chapter 1 of the book of Joshua, God told him to be strong and courageous. The third time, in verse 9, God added, "for the LORD your God will be with you wherever you go."

Be strong and courageous. The Lord your God will be with you.

Those words leaped off the page and slapped me across the cheek! *Holy cow!* I said to myself.

I had heard of people saying they felt that they had received a word from the Lord, and this was the first time I had ever experienced that. I don't think I've felt a moment that strong since.

The message through those words was clear: *You need to go back and wrestle.*

For that reason, the story of Joshua still carries special meaning for me. I also take note of how Joshua stepped up and became an outstanding leader. The dude was a true warrior.

We need more Christian men to step up today and take on that warrior mentality.

A common picture of Jesus portrays Him as solemn and peaceful, with hands open in a non-threatening manner. But I like to picture the tough-as-nails Jesus who marched into the temple and started turning over the money-changers' tables.[5]

Christian men are portrayed far too often as weak, and I am tired of seeing us presented that way. We need more men who are tough mentally and emotionally. That's what warriors are.

I've described my physical toughness as a wrestler, and I can tell you from experience that wrestling injured and not quitting is a piece of cake compared with not quitting mentally and emotionally.

It wasn't easy to walk away from a well-paying job to come home and help raise my kids, because I worried about the finances. It wasn't easy to go back to wrestling after the lifestyle I had previously led

---

5   Accounts are included in all four Gospels. See Matthew 21:12–16, Mark 11:15–18, Luke 19:45–46, and John 2:13–16.

and say that I had become a Christian and that no matter what any-one thought, the new me was there to stay. It wasn't easy to get on the Internet and read people saying I had done horrible things after becoming a believer and know that even though what they were say-ing was untrue, I couldn't do anything to stop them. It wasn't easy to be made fun of for trying to live like a Christian. And it certainly wasn't easy to be hurt—sometimes repeatedly—by people I loved and cared for.

[handwritten marginal note: tracking on internet]

It is extremely difficult not to quit when you believe you are doing everything you are supposed to be doing, when you're doing things the right way, and you still get the shaft. So it encourages me to know that Jesus broke down when He was arrested in the garden of Gethsemane the night before His crucifixion. Matthew describes Jesus as "sorrowful and troubled." Mark says He was "deeply distressed and troubled." Luke says He was "in anguish" and "his sweat was like drops of blood falling to the ground."[6]

It wasn't easy for Jesus to fulfill His purpose, but He did, and I have salvation because of it.

Jesus didn't quit.

Warriors don't quit.

Real men don't quit.

The theme running throughout the Old Testament that stands out most to me is obedience. The warrior mentality of a real man finds its expression in obedience to God.

That can be a stumbling block for some, I suspect, because it is easy to think that being obedient makes you like a child. I've seen it in my own life. I'm a grown man, closing in on fifty. I hadn't realized it until my wife said it, but through my wrestling career I created an enterprise built on my name, so I can't remember the last time some-one told me I needed to be obedient to someone else. I could argue

---

6   Read the full accounts in Matthew 26:36–46, Mark 14:32–42, and Luke 22:39–53.

that I've earned the right to do what I want. Yet I gladly do what I can to walk in obedience to God.

If someone wants to tell me that such obedience makes me like a child, then I'll agree and tell him I am a child—a child of God!

Being obedient and being submissive doesn't make me any less of a man. It makes me a real man.

Becoming a real man changed me in both my professional and personal lives.

I went back to wrestling able to talk about anything. I could have conversations with other wrestlers in which I could admit I was afraid of failure. I wouldn't have been able to do that before. And I stopped defining my manhood by how many beers I could drink and pills I could take and still remain standing. Instead of waking up in the morning and wondering what had happened the night before, I got out of bed and ate breakfast with my wife and kids.

I allowed myself to dress up and act silly while taking my daughter out for a date every Valentine's Day, because it meant a lot to her. I might have taken her out for a Valentine's meal before, but I don't think you would have caught me all dressed up and acting silly.

My badge of honor used to come from my ability to deliver a one-hour match that thrilled fans. Now I wrestle my son for thirty minutes and have trouble winning, and that is far more satisfying.

I reflect back to when Rebecca and I closed our business and put our home and building up for sale. That entire situation required mental and emotional toughness for sure. And you know what? I didn't buckle, I didn't run, and my family was all the better for it.

Rebecca led our family when my life was out of control. Yet through the stress of our home and building not selling and facing debt, I took the lead with my family. That was one of those very tough times that most, if not all, of us encounter at some point that causes stress on a marriage, and then the stress on the marriage puts a strain on the entire family.

It was one of those times when the option enters your mind that maybe the best thing would be to pack up the tent and leave. Before

I came to Christ, that is probably what I would have decided to do. It would have been easy to rationalize that my leaving would have provided both Rebecca and me the opportunity to make fresh starts on our own. But that thinking would have been flawed. I knew that the best option for our family—for us as a whole and all of us individually—was for me to lead us through the struggle. That started with me, for the first time, truly putting our family's financial security in the Lord's hands and trusting that He would provide for us. Because I made that decision, I was able to lead my family in a way that I like to think would have made Joshua smile. I didn't know it until then, but God had been equipping me to be a man—a warrior—in tough times.

Before I was a Christian, my behavior was cocky and arrogant. It was all a show to hide my deep insecurities. Becoming a Christian made me confident in a way I had never been and made it possible for me to handle being made fun of for my faith. It made it possible for me to walk into Bible studies where everybody knew I was "*the* Shawn Michaels" and express my desire to live a life of total submission.

I'm okay with not being the focus. I'm okay with not being relevant. I'm okay with not being anything except a husband to Rebecca and a father to Cameron and Cheyenne, and to do a good job in those roles.

I pray that I live long enough to see my son become a father and to walk my daughter down the aisle. I want to play with my grandchildren and see them become decent, God-fearing people. That would be an accomplishment in itself in the world we live in now.

I am only interested in being looked at as "the man" if it means I'm being the man God wants me to be.

CHAPTER 11
POWER IN PARTNERSHIP

"Two are better than one, because they have a good return for their labor" (Ecclesiastes 4:9).

[handwritten: Better w/ a partner ring + life]

I am a whole lot tougher to beat when I have a great partner, whether in wrestling or in life.

In wrestling, sometimes you get to choose your partners, and sometimes they're chosen for you by promoters. Either way, the hope is to create a partnership that finds the chemistry like that of two actors in an unforgettable movie performance.

When two wrestlers find that chemistry, matches take on a natural flow. One will start to sling an opponent against the ropes across the ring, and his partner will know he's about to get tagged into the ring for a combo move on the opponent. Good tag-team partners don't have to look for each other, because they can sense where the other is. It's like a marriage when a spouse can complete the other's sentences. And when you find that kind of partner in wrestling, it's magic.

[handwritten margin note: Liken's a good Tag team partner to a good wife]

Much of my success in wrestling came from my early partnership with Marty Jannetty. I met Marty during my short stint in Kansas City. Bill Watts sent me from Mid-South to Central States Wrestling,

[handwritten: Marty Jannetty]

and Marty was one of the first wrestlers I met there. Marty was two-and-a-half years older than me and had made his wrestling debut a few months ahead of mine. He had already established himself as a baby-face—one of the good guys—at CSW. Marty and Dave Peterson invited me to ride to shows with them, saying they saw potential in me as a wrestler and wanted to help me out.

Being friends outside of the ring is no guarantee of a tag team's potential inside the ring, and when Marty and I were paired together before a match, there was nothing to suggest that we could be onto something big.

But once inside the ring, we instantly clicked. We seemed to know what each other's next move was going to be, and from a timing standpoint it felt as if we had been working together for months. We both recognized that we had that sought-after chemistry, but I was on my way out of CSW.

I was making only $250–$350 per week in Kansas City, and after a couple of months there, Jose Lothario called and asked if I would like to come back to San Antonio to wrestle. Jose and Fred Behrend had taken over Southwest Championship Wrestling and renamed it Texas All-Star Wrestling. When Jose offered me $500 per week guaranteed, I was headed back to San Antonio only nine months into my career to be promoted as the hometown boy made good.

In Texas I was paired with Paul Diamond as the American Force. Paul and I proved to be a good match, and we had a good run going when Jose, who was always looking out for me, told me I needed to go bigger and suggested I send out tapes of my wrestling to a couple of larger organizations.

I was in San Antonio for less than a year when the American Wrestling Alliance, which had its matches broadcast on ESPN, offered me a job. AWA had also hired Marty. After I wrestled twice as a single, AWA co-founder Verne Gagne told Marty and me that he wanted us to become a tag team. The Midnight Rockers were born.

As a Christian, I don't believe in coincidence. I believe that, unbeknownst to me at the time, God's hand was in that pairing.

Marty and I had no idea what lay ahead of us as a tag team, but we were pumped about working together and jumped into the assignment with all four of our feet. We decided we wanted to bring a new brand of excitement to wrestling. We talked about other tag teams we had watched and felt that too many of them failed to operate *as a team*. They looked like two different styles of wrestlers who just tagged each other into the ring. We wanted to place more emphasis on the team aspect of a tag team. We wanted to maintain an up-tempo style in the ring and complement each other by doing a lot of double moves.

We tried that, and it worked really well. We grew big in a hurry, and Marty and I were hired away by Vince McMahon and his then-WWF. We got fired after a few weeks there and went to wrestle out of Birmingham, Alabama. From there, we moved on to Memphis, Tennessee, and wound up wrestling in that territory and also for the American Wrestling Association for a while.

Eventually we received a second chance with Vince's company. I learned years later that after we had left WWF, Pat Patterson would ask Vince almost every month if Marty and I could be brought back. Each time, Vince would say no. Finally, after about a year of Pat asking, Vince relented, but warned Pat, "It's all on you. They are your responsibility. They're on probation here."

Vince had us drop "Midnight" from our name so we would have a different name than when we were with the AWA, and the Rockers had a highly successful run until we split up in late 1991.

I am of the opinion that events look different through the lens of history than they do at the time they occur. Marty and I received a lot of praise when we were together, but history is telling us that we were even better than the credit we were given. We were innovative and had a major role in changing the style of tag-team wrestling.

We also had a strong partnership outside of matches. A bit older than I was, Marty had a better ability to adjust to changes and sort out the business issues of our sport. He took the lead on the business side of our partnership. We made good decisions along the way, but we also made bad decisions. Because Marty took the lead does not mean our mistakes were more his fault than mine. We were in things together.

Marty and I brought out the best in each other inside the ring, and we brought out the worst in each other outside the ring. That followed us for many years—long after we stopped wrestling as tag-team partners—and precipitated my slow spiral into a world I never knew about and was quite curious about. I was enjoying my first taste of success.

Back then, that way of living seemed like the thing to do. I know better now, of course. Obviously, things have changed in my life, and I can look back now and see how both of us were young and dumb.

I took on the nickname "The Heartbreak Kid" when I launched a career separate from Marty. Vince and Pat chose to make "Sensational Sherri" (Sherri Martel) my manager, although I wasn't big on having one. I had just come from a long run in a tag team, and having a manager seemed to me like it would be more of the same.

Pat Patterson explained that Sherri had worked with "Macho Man" Randy Savage, Ted DiBiase, and others who routinely wrestled in main events.

"She is going to elevate you," Pat told me.

That stung a little bit, because I was thinking that I had become pretty big and would do well on my own. It wasn't that I didn't want to work with Sherri; it was that bringing someone on to partner with me didn't seem like the big break I was anticipating. I didn't make a big stink about it, but I did put up a little resistance.

Sherri and I talked, and she was unbelievably wonderful and supportive from the start. It turned out to be a great decision to pair me with her, because Sherri provided a big boost to what had started from my teaming with Marty.

My next partner was Kevin Nash. Kevin was the first partner that I had chosen. I had watched Kevin in WCW, where he had wrestled under the names Steel, Oz, and Vinnie Vegas. As Vinnie Vegas he had an Andrew Dice Clay swagger about him that cracked me up.

Kevin Nash

I thought Kevin was a riot. He was huge, too—6-foot-10, close to 300 pounds—and I thought it would be smart to bring him aboard as a ringside bodyguard character for me.

I was Intercontinental Champion at the time, and we had fallen into the rut of having matches ended by disqualifications. They wanted me to keep the belt, but because I was a young, cocky, smaller, bad guy, I was the type of wrestler who would best be used to make the good guys look good. The only way we could fulfill both needs was to have the good guy do something dastardly to get disqualified and lose the match—and then beat me up to leave the fans happy. The matches grew redundant. I needed someone with me who could help me get an out, who could help me cheat to win and keep the title. If I could win by cheating, I could cause more people to dislike me and get more heat on me.

Using big Kevin as a bodyguard seemed like a creative way to make that happen.

Rick Steiner had previously wrestled with WCW, so I asked if he knew Vinnie Vegas. They just so happened to be good friends. Rick called Kevin with my idea, and Kevin told him that he was under contract to WCW, but would see what he could do.

The next day Kevin called Rick and asked him to have someone from WWE call him. Vince called, and the next week at *Raw*, Kevin debuted as my bodyguard under the name "Diesel."

Kevin became Diesel

Kevin and I had never talked until he came to WWE, but we hit it off right away. Kevin was a hysterically funny dude, and I love to laugh. His sense of humor filled a void in my life, because I was going through a time when I wasn't happy with myself and needed someone to give me reasons to laugh.

As with Marty, Kevin and I brought out the best of each other as wrestlers, but also the worst of each other outside of wrestling.

Like Marty, good + bad for each other

We eventually became a tag team known as Two Dudes with Attitudes and had a couple of great runs together from 1993 to 1995, and then we reunited after my return when I joined the nWo stable.

After Kevin, I partnered with Paul Levesque, who wrestled as

Hunter Hearst Helmsley, or Triple H, whom I met at *WrestleMania 11*, in 1995, shortly after Hunter had joined WWF.

Hunter started hanging around my circle of friends—Kevin, Scott Hall, and Kid (Sean Waltman). We were such a tight group that the other wrestlers starting calling us The Kliq. That name wasn't always used in flattering terms, because some viewed us as a group that held and wielded political power to get our way within the organization. Admittedly, we did have Vince's ear, we did exert influence, and what we pushed for was for the good of WWF.

It was a crucial time for WWF. The business was changing, and we faced the potential of getting our tails kicked by WCW if we did nothing or if we did the wrong things, because WCW was on the rise. We were the guys who had earned our spots at the top of the sport and had strong opinions about the direction WWF needed to take.

Hunter and I quickly became close friends, and we made up half of D-Generation X when it formed, along with bodyguard Chyna and Rick Rude. Not only did WWF benefit from what Hunter and I did in the ring, but it also was a good business move to keep us together because Hunter, who didn't drink and party, practically babysat me.

Hunter could still cause trouble professionally, which is part of what defined us as The Kliq. We made waves, but the bosses probably figured that we would make fewer waves if we were together. If I went off the rails drugs-wise—and that was a real threat—Hunter would be there with me. And then if we both went off the rails professionally, it would be easier to contain us if we were together.

DX did make the company a boatload of money.

Hunter stuck by me in the aftermath of the Montreal Screwjob. After the match, it was a little scary, because Bret Hart became extremely upset and started slamming TV monitors in the back, and I didn't know who all would side with him. The match was supposed to end—at least the way everyone thought it would end—with Hunter coming to the ring and interfering, causing chaos and ending the match with a disqualification. But we found a way to end the match before Hunter could become involved.

After the match, Hunter and Chyna were in my hotel room with me. It was one thing for me to talk about pulling a swerve, but it was altogether different to actually make it happen. We had no idea what the consequences would be, but the atmosphere behind the scenes in the arena afterward had been intimidating.

"You want me to sit here with you for a while?" Hunter asked.

"For a little bit, if you don't mind," I said.

The next day we decided that we would walk into the TV event together. It wasn't out of the realm of possibility for another wrestler or other wrestlers to jump us. It was that intense, with a pretend storyline becoming pretty real to those involved. Hunter and I decided that if anyone was going to get knocked out, it was going to be both of us. Nobody wants to get beaten up, but it is easier to get beat up with your buddy. Let's put it this way: When your head gets put in a vise and someone else puts his in there with yours, you don't ever forget what that person did for you.

When I came back from retirement, we worked an angle with Hunter and me as rivals. Hunter turned on me, and I won the World Heavyweight Championship from him and then dropped it back to him. Then, of course, there was our DX reunion after our return.

Hunter and I were the last ones from The Kliq still with WWE, because the rest had left for the rival WCW. We bonded even further over that. We feel that we sort of shared a foxhole together. We saw each other at our worst, and we saw each other at our best.

We are still very tight. Hunter is now an executive vice president at WWE. He married Vince's daughter, Stephanie (whom he had previously "married" as part of a storyline), and he eventually will be running that company.

When I was selected into the WWE Hall of Fame, I asked Hunter to introduce me at the induction ceremony. It pained him greatly to have to say something nice about me in his speech, because he would rather show that he cares about me by busting my chops.

Hunter was an awesome partner and remains an awesome friend.

The only time a pairing didn't appear natural in the ring, oddly enough, was with Jose Lothario. Early in my career, Vince thought Jose would spice up a storyline leading up to a *WrestleMania*, and he brought Jose in as my manager.

Jose still felt like a mentor to me, yet I had advanced far beyond that nineteen-year-old he had trained in San Antonio. I was uncomfortable being the guy who would determine how to use my mentor.

More problematic, I also had been playing a bad guy and then got switched to a goody-two-shoes character I didn't feel real good about doing. My character had left the last *WrestleMania* as a cocky guy with an attractive woman on his arm, and then I flipped to become a more humble character with an older man as my manager. It took me a while to step into that new role, and that made it challenging to know how best to utilize Jose. I didn't incorporate Jose enough, and the idea didn't pan out the way we had hoped.

Also, I didn't have the ability then that I do now to get things out in the open with people, so I couldn't ask Jose if he was upset with me or disappointed with me. Jose was from wrestling's old school—poker-faced and tight-lipped—and I couldn't get a read on how he felt about how we were doing.

Jose and I had a good relationship when he was training me, and Vince wanted that real-life aspect of my story to come through in the storyline. But with the drastic changes in my character, and with me not doing a good job of acting out that transition, the chemistry wasn't there with Jose's character, and our real-life relationship just didn't come through at all.

Tag-teaming with a friend doesn't guarantee chemistry, but I couldn't imagine having a tag-team partner I didn't become friends with, because you spend so much time together. I saw other tag teams who weren't buddies outside the ring, but I don't think I could have done that.

Wrestlers share a common bond that it seems to me would be like what soldiers share: They can go their separate ways and then come back together years later for a reunion and sit there and share that understanding of what they went through together in a way that others in the room can't understand. Wrestling, to me, feels like a body I am a part of, much like a church body.

Now I can look back at all those relationships and partnerships and see a pattern, and that brings me back to God. We cannot see from beginning to end the way He does, but from what I can make out in my rearview mirror, I can see that each relationship I developed along the way was like a narrowing path bringing me closer and closer to being in relationship with Him. Each one of those people taught me something about myself, and I didn't know it at the time, but reflecting on those relationships later would show me a lot about my ability to develop and maintain relationships.

―――――――――

By far, the best partner I have ever chosen is my wife, Rebecca.

I had been married once before. I don't talk about it publicly much, out of respect to my ex-wife. I was twenty-three at the time, and she was nineteen. We were married a short time when we realized that neither of us had been ready to marry, and we got an amicable divorce. The problem wasn't who I married, but my quick decision to marry and the person *I* was at that point in my life.

I was thirty-four when I married Rebecca. She was heaven-sent and the catalyst for all the wonderful changes in my life.

I can remember commenting very early in our relationship that even if I didn't marry Rebecca, she was a person I would want to hang around for the rest of my life. She instantly recognized that I hadn't had a lot of people like that in my life. She noted that because of my public career, I had to keep a guard up for people who wanted to be takers, whose motives I had to question to protect myself.

"I can see where that would be an issue in your life all the time," she told me. "What can I do to make sure I eliminate myself as being one of those people?"

That one question meant a lot to me.

She made it known that her goal was to be there for me. It's hard not to dig that!

Then, after we married, despite all the things I was doing, she never went down the nagging trail. She would have been well within her rights to nag, but she chose to go about it a different way.

If she had nagged me, I don't think it would have gone well. There were a couple of occasions when she had to set me straight, and I got defensive with her, even flat-out lying.

When Cameron was a baby, and before my salvation, we bought a computer. As I was learning how to use it, a buddy showed me some web sites. Yeah, those kinds.

Rebecca asked if I had been looking at porn.

"Nope," I said. I hadn't learned that it's possible to check the history of web sites that have been called up on a computer.

Rebecca asked again, and I denied again.

She called up the history list, and I had to admit what I had been doing.

Rebecca hadn't had many guys treat her as well as they should have. They all eventually seemed to disappoint her or hurt her. Because we hadn't dated long before marrying, there was much I had yet to learn about her, including her history with relationships. And here I was doing something that had to make her think I might be just like all the other guys who had hurt her.

She called my lawyer.

"I want a divorce," she told him.

"Well, Rebecca," he said, "I am Shawn's lawyer."

"I don't care," she replied. "I don't want anything. I just want a divorce."

My lawyer told her that they could talk more about it later. She left the house with Cameron for the night while hoping, I learned later, that I would come after her.

I didn't. I was stubborn.

Rebecca called
Lawyer — Divorce

She came back home the next day, and we had an open and honest discussion in which she helped me understand how much I had hurt her. That was a pivotal moment in our marriage. We saw—especially, I saw—that we had some growing to do in our relationship.

I was in the midst of all my bad stuff when that happened. In addition to the mental fogs I was in and out of because of the pills, I also didn't know as much about my wife as I should have. I didn't know enough about the human heart, either. I failed to recognize that I was hurting Rebecca.

It's embarrassing to admit that I was looking at pornography, but I know that porn is often a major issue for men, whether they're Christians or non-Christians. For me, the porn was just a curiosity, and my curiosity was no reflection on Rebecca. The problem was completely with me. That didn't change the fact, however, that I broke her heart. It certainly was unintentional, but I did.

I love Rebecca—always have loved her—and not wanting to break her heart again motivated me. I think she saw that even though it had to be a scary time for her. I told her I wouldn't look at porn again, and in the fifteen years since, I have stayed true to my promise. From that moment, we started down the road to strengthening our relationship.

There's one story about Rebecca that blows my mind when I think about it. Many of those nights when I was passed out on the couch, after she had rearranged my body to make sure my back was in a comfortable position, when she would go to our walk-in closet to pray that God would help me stop taking the pills, she would sense the Holy Spirit telling her these words: "You change. You be the woman you are supposed to be, and he will be the man he's supposed to be."

It still amazes me to think that instead of nagging me to make the obvious changes I needed to make, she set out to get her heart right with the Lord. Instead of pushing me into what she thought I needed to become, she handed me a study Bible and a couple of books so that the Holy Spirit could begin reshaping me into what *He* wanted me to be.

Married Rebecca 1998 ?

We had been married seven years when I wrote my first book. We have more than doubled that now. We've had more time to withstand the challenges married couples go through. We've had more time to struggle and to make mistakes. We've had battles to endure. (Does anyone want to buy an empty building in San Antonio?)

If I had continued to love Rebecca the same way as I had before I got saved, I don't think our marriage would have survived what we've endured over the years. I would have probably bailed because I didn't understand the importance of the family and what my role was as husband and father.

To love Rebecca the way she needed to be loved, I had to become a better partner to her.

It took me a while to figure out what makes her tick. That's not to imply I know everything about her. Gosh, no. But I do have a better grasp of how she thinks and what is important to her.

About ten years into our marriage, I learned through *The Five Love Languages* book written by Gary Chapman that Rebecca is a service-oriented person. If I want to show her that I love her, the best way is by doing things for her. I could buy her a dozen roses, and I don't think she could care less. But when I unload the dishwasher, then I'm the man!

I am not a service-oriented guy. I don't like unloading the dishwasher. It's not a natural response for me to see a full dishwasher and go put all the dishes in the cabinets. I don't equate unloading a dishwasher with an expression of appreciation. But Rebecca does. So when I want to show Rebecca that I love and appreciate her, I need to unload the dishwasher. (I have the feeling that previous sentence is going to get read back aloud and used against me frequently!)

We have both read enough books to understand that maintaining a joyful, positive environment in our home is one of the best things we can do for our children.

The best book — the Bible — contains what is known as the

"Love Chapter." It's 1 Corinthians 13, and in that chapter Paul defines love this way:

> Love is patient, love is kind. It does not envy, it does not boast, it is not proud. It does not dishonor others, it is not self-seeking, it is not easily angered, it keeps no record of wrongs. Love does not delight in evil but rejoices with the truth. It always protects, always trusts, always hopes, always perseveres.[7]

I've heard that in that biblical description of love, there's not much mention of feelings. What love *does* is more prominent that what loves *feels*. That's opposite of the way our society tends to define love. The reasons that Rebecca and I married have evolved into something much bigger and greater, even though the path has included bumps and pitfalls.

Knowing biblical truths has kept our marriage solid no matter what we have encountered. Obviously, it helps when we see some fruit from those biblical truths, because if you don't get some glimpses of hope, it's hard to keep going.

I'm pretty good at handling just about anything if I have a little bit of hope. I'm a lot like Jim Carrey's dim-witted Lloyd Christmas character in the movie *Dumb and Dumber*. He asks the wealthy and attractive Mary Swanson, played by Lauren Holly, if there's a chance that a guy like him would end up with a girl like her. She says the chances are not good.

"You mean, not good like one out of a hundred?" he follows up.

"I'd say more like one out of a million," she responds.

Lloyd pauses a few seconds before saying, "So you're telling me there's a chance? Yeah!"

That's me. As long as there is any kind of chance, that's all I need to soldier on.

Rebecca and I can see fruit in our children. They are respectful. They recognize right and wrong, and they recognize sin. They openly

---

7 1 Corinthians 13:4–7.

and comfortably talk about God in public, and they think it's only natural to do so. That's nice to observe as a parent.

We can see fruit in our individual lives and in our marriage, too. We have been married for fifteen years now, and our relationship still is based on friendship and includes a lot of humor and a lot of joy. We still have love and dedication and passion for one another. That helps our faith, and it helps with our strength and endurance. It keeps us pushing on, moving on, and continuing to walk with God like Abram (before his name changed to Abraham), when the Lord appeared to him and said, "Walk before me faithfully."[8]

The Lord's instruction was not to run. It was to walk, and to do so faithfully. It was just step by step. I can reflect back on my marriage to Rebecca and see that we have grown together step by step through both the good and the bad. And I think that is an awesome kind of love to share.

8   Genesis 17:1.

CHAPTER 12
MENTORS SEEK TO SERVE

"As iron sharpens iron, so one person sharpens another"
(Proverbs 27:17).

Jose

———————

Mentors played vital roles in the beginnings of both my wrestling career and my Christian walk. When I had become experienced in both, I took advantage of opportunities to share what I had learned so that others could reap the same benefits I did.

Of course, my list of wrestling mentors begins with Jose, who trained me and set me on the path to realizing my dream of becoming a professional wrestler. Jose, in his old-school style, didn't waste a lot of time. He thought the best way to teach me was to put me in a ring and have me wrestle, which I did against a guy named Ken Johnson. I learned under Jose by doing.

Jose was an early believer in my abilities. Although Jose was in his late forties, he still was wrestling a little, and he let me drive him to and from matches in Houston so he could introduce me to some of the guys in Mid-South Wrestling. Jose wasn't a big talker, but he didn't mind letting people know that he was training me and that I would one day be a champion.

Jose gave me my ring name, convinced me to learn the backflip,

Jose influences

helped me choose what I would wear in the ring, and then used his connection with Bill Watts to land me a spot in Mid-South.

More mentors

Then, once I joined Mid-South, Ricky Morton, Robert Gibson, and Terry Taylor became mentors. In addition to letting me ride with them to matches so they could spend time teaching me about the sport, they also watched my matches and offered feedback. Having their instruction was huge, and I applied the input they gave me. They were willing to take time to answer questions or share their observations of my matches.

They would emphasize the importance of a good guy, especially, showing emotion and fire when making a comeback in a match. That was an important lesson, because early on, when nobody was cheering for me and I could hear a pin drop during my matches, I had to learn through the experienced wrestlers' advice to carry myself as if I was turning in the greatest match ever and was thrilled to be there. That was not easy. The tendency for young wrestlers is to wait to respond to the fans' reactions. But the unknown wrestler has to be able to display that emotion first, even when the fans don't know who he is or don't care about his match.

At the beginning of my career, it was cool to see how each town, each opponent, and each match were noticeably different. I would wrestle a guy one night and get advice from him, and then the next night we would wrestle in a different town and he would point out something else to me. Through my mentors I began to realize that every step in the process offered an opportunity to improve and build on.

became a mentor

After I had been in wrestling for a few years, I took on a mentoring role too. It would sound noble and applause-worthy to say that I chose to mentor because I viewed it as a way to give back to my sport. But honestly, I mentored because that was a natural part of the wrestling culture. I wanted to give back to my sport, sure, but I didn't have to choose to do so. I had been mentored coming up in the business, and becoming a mentor just seemed like the natural thing to do. I loved wrestling and wanted it to continue to prosper, so I did exactly as had been done for me and shared with the younger wrestlers what I had learned, both from others and through my own experiences.

That being said, I was a much better mentor after my first retirement. My presentation, to use Jim Ross's word, frequently lacked tact in my first stint, and I alienated much of the locker room. With the turnover that took place during my absence, I returned to an interesting mix of younger wrestlers. Some knew about my career, knew about my top matches, and, unfortunately, knew of my reputation. Others didn't really know who I was. I liked becoming familiar with both groups.

[handwritten margin note: People didn't like me]

I could discern which ones were most interested in learning everything they could about our sport. I could tell them, when the sport got hard and they battled frustration, that it was perfectly natural in our sport. It was enjoyable answering their questions, especially the ones about the business. And then there were times when I interjected my unsolicited advice when I saw guys doing things that were going to hurt their chances of becoming successful.

[handwritten margin note: become Mentor]

The young guys used to make me laugh because when some of them would get into the ring with me, I could see this "You're Shawn Michaels!" look in their eyes, and I would have to yell at them during the match, "Hit me!"

One trait I admired about the new generation of wrestlers was that they didn't seem to completely identify themselves with the sport the way my generation did. They had identities outside of wrestling. Another way of putting it is that they had a life. Some of the older guys were bothered by that, because they thought the young guys appeared as though they didn't care as much as we had at their age. There were peers who thought the young guys were lazy and didn't love wrestling. My observation was that either things didn't bother them as much as us or they possessed a better ability to roll with whatever happened to them. The young guys weren't as controlled by the sport as we had been. They had hobbies and interests outside of the wrestling, and I thought that was beneficial for their careers and lives.

Wrestlers haven't been dropping over dead on a regular basis as

Wrestlers dying young

they did during my wrestling days. I knew too many wrestlers who had died from drugs. There were others who died in unfortunate mishaps and from natural health reasons. I don't want to lump all the wrestlers who died during my era into one group who died from making bad choices, but the partying lifestyle, of which I was a full participant, cut short lives. That lifestyle doesn't seem to be as prevalent among today's wrestlers.

I don't hear as much as I used to about wrestlers getting involved in bar fights and getting arrested. I'm not as in the loop as I used to be, but those types of issues don't seem to come up as often now. Plus, WWE has done a good job of taking steps to protect the wrestlers, especially with regard to head injuries, by keeping trainers on hand and taking advantage of technological advances in medicine. The wrestlers and wrestling are healthier today for all of the above reasons.

I encouraged the younger guys to develop a balance between wrestling and their outside lives. The powers that be expected wrestlers to focus on their careers 24/7. For those who were young and single and intent on working their way up the ladder, I advised them to devote more time to the sport. But at the same time, I told them never to let anyone make them feel bad about having hobbies and activities outside of wrestling. I wanted them to know that it's smart to take three days completely off. Instead of watching films of matches or working out in a ring when they're supposed to be off, I encouraged them to go to the beach with their wives or girlfriends, or go fishing. I had learned there's an upside to maintaining a balance, and the way I maintained that balance was to work hard on WWE time and then go home and enjoy my family on my time.

That was advice I had not been given by anyone inside the business. As a result, I made things twice as difficult on myself as they needed to be. It's a hard enough job anyway. Wrestling was my life and the focus of everything I did. Nobody complained about the lifestyle back then, even though it came with a tough grind, because we were doing what we wanted to do.

The bottom line on what I shared with the new guys when I

Should have a life outside wrestling.

returned was that it is okay to have a life. I knew those who had a life outside of wrestling faced ridicule and pressure to be like the others in the way wrestling had always been, but I didn't want them to forget that it is good to have a little normalcy in their lives.

I was blessed to have strong spiritual mentors around me back home and when I returned to wrestling.

Two Christian wrestlers, Ted DiBiase and Tully Blanchard, my boyhood idol from San Antonio, both made themselves available to me when I rejoined WWE.

Tully + Ted helped after return

I was wrong about this, but I felt certain that no one outside of wrestling would be able to relate to the severity of my sins. I would hear people at church talk about how bad their lifestyles were before they became Christians and my reaction would be, *Oh, please! You guys don't know the half of it.* Surely nobody had lived a lifestyle close to mine.

Wrong! I eventually heard some of their stories and was surprised how I could look at people in their current state and have no idea of the way they had previously lived.

It took me a while to learn that, but fortunately I had Ted and Tully to turn to with my questions. They gave me sort of a Christianity for Dummies-styled education. They both helped me view things from a Christian perspective and also gave me tips on how to put my Christianity into practice, especially in the wrestling environment. It was Tully who gave me the great advice to start reading the Bible in the Gospels and read them repeatedly to familiarize myself with the story and life of Jesus.

I never hesitated to reach out to Ted and Tully, and I can't remember either of them ever not taking time to help me. They were only a phone call away.

Always there for me

Fortunately, I also had two people locally who were always available to me, Keith and Priscilla Parker. Keith was the Cornerstone staff member who had invited me to his Bible study the day I walked unannounced into the church office.

Keith and Priscilla were exactly the kind of folks to which every

Locals

new Christian should have access. They had more to do with my Christian walk getting off to a good, solid start than anyone else. It pains me to hear of someone who gets saved and then has no one there to help him. Discipleship — teaching and showing others, especially newer believers, how to live the Christian life — should never be overlooked by those of us who have been Christians for a while. Without it, new Christians are left out there alone and without direction, whereas it is through discipleship that Christians mature and make an impact on the people around them. That is what makes churches healthy and growing.

Keith and Priscilla talked to me about setting aside quiet time alone for prayer and studying the Bible. Keith, especially, had a way of giving me simple, direct, concise directions. I was an athlete, and I was accustomed to following directions. Give me a game plan, and I'll execute it. That's what Keith did for me.

The Parkers quickly became really good friends whom I (and Rebecca) could ask anything at any time. Keith and Priscilla earned my trust, and that was important. They were not influenced in the least by my status as a wrestler. They cared about Shawn Hickenbottom, not Shawn Michaels.

One unfortunate price of my celebrity is that I always feel I'll need to gauge people's sincerity: Are they more into the wrestler or into the person I am when I'm out of character? I've met people who no doubt were wonderful and genuine, but when they would start asking more about wrestling than my personal life, I felt I needed to draw a line that kept our relationship from growing too close.

My mom used to tell me that as long as I had five people in my life whom I could call on whenever I needed them, I would be in good shape. When you're a public figure, the number of people who could take on that role of confidant dwindles significantly. That's tough, because from a faith standpoint you need people around you with whom you can confidently get into some pretty deep and vulnerable areas.

Providing fellowship is an important function of the church, but

I'm the type of person who doesn't need more than a few people in my innermost circle. Keith and Priscilla were in that circle because they were trustworthy. I could reveal to them my deepest secrets. I could tell them I needed prayer for a specific need, share the details with them, and not have to worry that my need would make the rounds at church. That's something that can be a problem in churches. There have been people who asked if there was anything I wanted them to pray for, and because I couldn't trust them, I answered, "Nope," even if I did have a need. That's not only true for someone who is a recognized figure, such as I've been; it's also true for other people in churches.

We need to be able to express the areas in which we need help and ask our brothers and sisters to do as the Bible instructs and bear those burdens with us by lifting us up in prayer. And then stop right there and not let it become fodder for rumors and gossip. The church needs to be the *first* place people — believers and non-believers — can safely go with their needs, not the last.

Although the Parkers moved back to Alabama two or three years after I became a Christian, we have continued to stay in close contact. I don't know how I would have made it through my early days as a Christian without the Parkers, and I have leaned on them throughout the process of trying to sell that empty building. I'm confident God could have provided other people to fulfill the role the Parkers have played in my life, but I surely am glad He sent Keith and Priscilla to mentor me.

Philip Fortenberry's bio on the Cornerstone website describes him as "Pastor, Counselor, Teacher, Minister, Public Speaker, Author, Survivalist, Outdoor Adventurer and Former Green Beret." That's a long list, but there is one important word missing: Friend.

Philip was the one who brought me into a role as spiritual mentor that became an incredibly rewarding experience for me.

Before I decided to go back to wrestling, I had contemplated finding a job with a church to be involved with a ministry that helped young boys. I had watched a story on the news that included alarming statistics about boys from single-parent homes. And then, of course, there were all those books I had read, including Dr. Dobson's, that emphasized how much boys miss out on when they're not around godly men.

I started keeping notes for how I could be a positive influence for boys missing that man in their lives. That is where my dream of owning a ranch began. If Rebecca and I could move to a ranch, I decided, I would be able to host those boys for little excursions on which I could take them hunting and fishing and teach them how to field dress a deer and how to cook in the outdoors—while talking to them about God.

Not too long after I started compiling ideas, I met a man in his mid-twenties at church and shared with him what I was thinking. He liked the ideas, and we started talking about putting together something small on our own.

Pastor Hagee and his son, Matt, who was on the pastoral staff, heard about our plans and decided to build a ministry at the church built around outdoors and single-parent boys. Philip was the guy they brought in to start the ministry.

It was about that time that I made the decision to go back to WWE. Still, Philip allowed me to help be a part of launching the ministry, and I took part in a hiking trip in Colorado that turned out well. One night we were all sitting around a campfire, and Philip gave his testimony. Then I gave mine. Philip's story was closer to what the boys were living through, because he had grown up without a father around. Of course, my story proved that you can have a dad around and still screw up your life.

Despite the differences in Philip's and my backgrounds, seeing a former Green Beret and a professional wrestler open up like we did made it easier for the boys to share their stories with one another. That was the beginning of the healing process for a lot of those boys.

Over time, Philip began to see that it wasn't enough to reach out to the boys. Their mothers also needed to be equipped to raise the boys as single parents. That led to some changes in that ministry at the church, and one day Philip came to me and said he no longer could lead the Thursday night Bible study for the boys. He said the boys wanted to keep the Bible study going and asked if I would take over.

I jumped on that opportunity. It fit nicely into my schedule, because I could lead the boys on Thursday nights and then fly out on Fridays to be with WWE.

The appeal of keeping the Bible study going for the boys was obvious. For me personally it also met a need, because I was concerned that with my return to wrestling I could get out of touch with my desire to be of service.

When God puts something on my heart, I have to do it. Since I had heard those statistics on the news, God had been laying that type of ministry on my heart, and I couldn't rest until I saw it come to life.

We kept that group of boys together all the way through their high school graduations and into college for a few. I still hear from some of the boys from time to time. Not too long ago, one texted to ask, "If you screw up, do you mess up God's will or is that a part of God's will?"

Another recently texted to say that his grandmother, who was Catholic, was in the hospital and he wanted to visit her and pray with her. But he said he didn't know any Catholic prayers. I texted back that his going to see her and pray with her as he knew how would mean the world to her. Then I told him that if he wasn't sure where his grandmother stood with Jesus, he should ask her. If she said she hadn't accepted Christ as her Savior, then he could have that conversation with her.

It's really cool that after all those years, after we had all gone our separate ways, the guys can text me to ask questions that are important to them — much like my mentors have done for me.

I took over the group for the boys' sake, but when you allow God to use you in an area He places in your heart, when you intentionally seek to serve others, you can't help but be encouraged and strengthened in your faith too.

CHAPTER 13
FREEDOM IN FORGIVENESS

"Bear with each other and forgive one another if any of you has a grievance against someone. Forgive as the Lord forgave you" (Colossians 3:13).

Forgiveness is one of the main themes of the Bible, and without it I would not be where I am today. Forgiveness also is at the heart of the wrestling story with which I am most associated. The two are connected.

The Montreal Screwjob remains the biggest controversy in the history of wrestling. If a bigger one comes along, I'll feel sorry for the guys involved. It's no fun being the bad guy in a story like that.

Bret Hart and I had been pretty good friends in my early days in WWE. We were the smaller guys, but felt like we were the future of the company. We foresaw a day when WWE would focus more on wrestling ability instead of just being big. So that was something we had bonded over.

But for more than twelve years after the match in Montreal, the relationship between Bret and me was nonexistent. Bret left WWE for WCW, and we didn't talk to each other during that time period. We didn't exchange a text or an email.

I would occasionally hear of something Bret had said about me in an interview, and none of it was good. Later, Bret was one of those who questioned my Christianity when I got back into the sport. (I became a Christian five years after our rivalry reached its climax.)

My anger over what took place in Montreal didn't last nearly as long as Bret's, which was understandable, because Bret was the one who felt that he had been wronged.

The path toward our reconciliation probably began in 2006 when Bret was inducted into the WWE Hall of Fame. By that point, I was over everything and ready to put the situation behind us. I didn't think he was ready for that, though, because of what I was hearing him say in interviews.

I can't remember who it was, but someone told me that Bret wouldn't want me to attend the Hall of Fame induction. But I was going. He was one of seven inductees that year, including my former manager Sensational Sherrie and my friend Eddie Guerrero, who had passed away five months earlier.

I insisted I would go. It was suggested that I not sit front and center during the ceremony. I was fine with that. Just to tell you how crazy it got over our feud, there were numerous reports that I left before Bret was inducted. Some reports said I walked out; others said I was told to leave. All were untrue. I stayed for the entire ceremony; it's just that I wasn't in a visible spot.

After the final induction, I was leaving when I came upon some of Bret's family. I talked briefly with the family, and they were all very nice and pleasant to me.

One of Bret's nieces, Nattie Niedhart, was working in WWE and later became well known as one of WWE's Divas. Oddly enough, she had been a Shawn Michaels fan when she was younger. Nattie and I would talk from time to time, and I got to know her boyfriend, Tyson Kidd. Tyson had been trained by Bret and came to WWE in 2009 as part of The Hart Dynasty. Nattie was Tyson's manager, and they were a really sweet couple who wound up marrying in 2013.

As Nattie and Tyson became more active in WWE, we talked

more frequently. In one conversation, Bret's name came up, and I said that I wished we could put everything behind us someday. That was the extent of it.

Then several weeks later, out of the blue, Tyson said that Bret had told him that he was ready to hash things out too. Tyson said Bret had asked him to give me Bret's phone number in case I ever wanted to talk to him.

That was probably in late summer of 2009. About that same time, we began to hear rumblings of Bret possibly returning to WWE in some regard. Every time that possibility came up, I was asked if I thought it would work for both of us to be in WWE together.

I always answered that it would be fine with me. I was willing to do whatever I could to help if he and WWE both wanted to get back together. He could have beaten me up and put me in his Sharpshooter, whatever they wanted. Heck, I would have screamed like a little girl if they asked me to. That's one of those changes resulting from becoming a Christian. I'd previously had strong opinions about how I should have been used on the television shows, but by then I didn't really care. They could have put me in diapers and made me suck my thumb. If that was the role they wanted me to play that week because that was the best thing for the company, I'd happily do it and the next morning take my flight home.

I want to give Bret credit for reaching out to me. He texted me first, and that started an open line of texting between us. We didn't talk over the phone, but we did start communicating. I expressed my willingness to do what I could to help make his comeback better. At one point I told Bret that I would love to talk to him, but if he didn't want to, I would understand. He responded that it would be a good idea for us to get together when we could.

I think it was December 2009 when Bret re-signed with WWE, and they planned to bring him back as part of a feud with Vince and have him make his return in the first Monday night *Raw* of the new year. We knew we would have our first chance to talk that Monday.

A lot of time had passed since Montreal — a little more than

12 years had passed

twelve years—and I could sense a little something there in advance of meeting with Bret. I couldn't precisely identify what it was. Maybe "discomfort" is the best way to describe it. I think most of that stemmed from not knowing how Bret was going to respond, but I knew for sure I was ready to finally find closure.

The first time I saw Bret was in the large lunch room that Monday in Dayton, Ohio. There were a number of people there, but when I entered the room, I spotted Bret eating at a table with his back to me. If I remember correctly, Nattie and Tyson were sitting with him.

I wasn't nervous at all as I made my way across the room toward Bret. I was hopeful that our conversation would go well based on the tone of our texts, but I was curious about how he would respond to seeing me, considering how long it had been since we had last been in the same room together.

I walked up behind Bret, placed my hand on his shoulder, and said hello to him.

Finally "Hey, Shawn," he said, and we shook hands. It was nice and felt net good.

2008 The lunch room wasn't the place for us to have our talk, and I told Bret I would like to meet when we could. He said he didn't want to talk about the TV segment for that night.

"No, no," I said. "Just you and me. I just want us to be able to sit and talk."

Bret said that was a good idea and suggested we talk after I had eaten.

After lunch we went off to Vince's office, and I apologized for the Montreal incident. The best I can recall, I told Bret, "I understand that you have heard about all the stuff that has gone on with me. Whether you believe it or you don't, I want you to know that I get how difficult that was for you, and I'm sorry for it. I hope you can forgive me. Even if you don't, I will go out there and try to make this the best segment I can. I will do absolutely anything you want. We don't have to be best friends. We don't have to be anything if you want, but I want you to know that I take responsibility for all the stuff

154

that I put you through, and I am sorry for it and do hope that you can forgive me."

Bret then talked for a couple of minutes and took responsibility for his role in the situation. It was a really nice conversation. We spent probably an hour together. We didn't discuss Montreal all that time, because we would trail off into other subjects like our families as we caught up from our twelve years of separation.

One topic neither of us wanted to talk about, however, was the segment. We didn't want to plan anything beyond the basics of who would be where and when. We both wanted to wing it so that it could come across as real of a moment as possible.

We did, though, assure each other that we both were on the up and up. That was important, because we had a long history of jabbing each other and neither of us would give an inch back in those days. But we both were crystal clear that none of that was going to happen this time. We had to trust each other, and I think both of us communicating that our intentions were pure put us in a good place before that night's meeting on TV.

The segment began with Bret in the ring. He addressed the fans for a bit and then asked for me to come from backstage to the ring. We stood almost toe-to-toe, and Bret told me he wanted to bury the hatchet and offer a truce. I turned and walked around the ring to contemplate Bret's offer. I walked back so that we were looking each other in the eyes again and could tell from the crowd's response that the fans were really eating this up.

I told Bret that he deserved what he got in Montreal and admitted I was in on Vince's swerve. I don't think the fans knew what to expect at that point. When I said, "And there's a part of me—there's a big part of me—that doesn't regret a bit of it," that elicited a loud chorus of boos along with some cheers. But then I started to soften my tone, leading to my telling Bret that he wasn't the only one who wanted to bury the hatchet.

"I guess all I have to say," I concluded, "is are you sure? And are you ready?"

Bret played it up very well for the crowd, said some nice things about me, and then offered his right hand in friendship. I thought for a few seconds and then extended my hand to his. We shook hands, and the fans went berserk.

The handshake was planned. Beyond that, we were going to play off the crowd's reaction and do what felt right to us in the ring. I started to leave the ring, but stopped and looked to the crowd. Out of the corner of my eyes, I could see Bret, to the right, turn to face me. I spun on my heels, quickly walked to Bret, and gave him one of those one-arm dude hugs. He embraced me also, with both of us patting the other on the back.

"The Hug" was real and heartfelt.

The most important thing to me has been our level of communication since that night. Bret and I are not best friends; we never were. But from that night on, we've continued to communicate with each other. We text each other frequently. Around the holidays, we will text each other Christmas greetings. Bret came to my last match, and we talked there. It meant a lot to me that he came to be a part of that night. We have made a few joint appearances, participated in a number of interviews and Q&As together, and we were part of a DVD about WWE's greatest rivalries.

"Cathartic" is the word Bret has often used to describe our reconciliation. That's a good summary, I think, not only for me, but also for fans. There was deep anger and bitterness from fans on both sides. That night in Dayton, I couldn't help but once again picture myself as a fifteen-year-old wrestling fan. There were fans in the arena and watching all around the world on television who were about fifteen years old when they watched the Montreal Screwjob take place. It staggered me to think that some of those fans were dads now, watching with their sons and telling them about the legend of Montreal, and how we had hated each other and were becoming friends again.

That night was one moment when real life and wrestling merged in a powerful manner. And if the story of Bret Hart and Shawn

Michaels—in real life and in the ring—is not the epitome of forgiveness and what forgiveness brings, I don't know what is.

That storyline featured drama and emotions that we rarely aimed for in wrestling because it was risky. It was part of that depth of story I was able to bring to wrestling after becoming a Christian. That came from having an ability to think and feel in ways I didn't have before.

As a result, the make-believe world of wrestling, with all its Spandex and hair spray, served as the stage for the real-life story of two guys who had a bitter rivalry wrestling hadn't seen before and hasn't seen since. Then our story came full circle, and we became friends again.

[handwritten margin note: Fake Story turned into Something Real!]

Untold numbers of fans were touched by our story of forgiveness because Bret and I were sincerely touched in our lives.

I don't know how anyone could argue that the Almighty God was not working in that.

Forgiveness brings freedom.

I choke up when I think about the depth of forgiveness God has given me. I was a sinner, born into sin. I turned into someone who, for all intents and purposes, I probably shouldn't have become. I was raised pretty well in a good, loving family—all of whom now are Christians. I was taught right from wrong.

My downward spiral began with curiosity. I was the good boy wondering what the other way of living was like, and the opportunity to find out came when I was on my own in a business that has its own unique seductive nature. That was a bad combination.

[handwritten margin note: I was a good boy who went Bad!]

It all started out as having fun. Like all sin, before I knew it, I was in so deep that I couldn't remember how I had gotten there or how to get out. I could make a lot of excuses, but the truth is that I didn't recognize my life as sinful. "Sin" wasn't a word I would have used to describe what I was doing.

In my mind, it was my life and I wasn't hurting anyone else. That was incorrect, of course, but that's what I believed. I knew I was

Daddy's Tired ⚡⚡

hurting myself, but because I didn't like myself, it didn't matter. My wife, my parents, my family, my friends—they were all hurt by what I was doing. I just didn't recognize it. When people are in the middle of following a life of sin, I'm not sure they can. They need some type of external jolt to wake them up. My jolt came that Friday night on the couch, when my son crawled up on me and said, "Daddy's tired." For the first time, I realized my potential to hurt others.

Sometimes I hear that people reject God out of fear of what they would have to give up. When I look at my life back then through the perspective of my life now, how could I not want to give up that death-dealing way of living?

There are two types of freedom, the way I see it.

The first freedom—the one that some don't want to give up—is the freedom that says, "God gave me a free will. I'm an American citizen, and I have the right to [fill in the blank]."

I'll be honest: Becoming a Christian requires giving up some rights. It requires giving up some freedom. And that's where that second type of freedom comes in.

The second kind of freedom—the one that only God can provide—brings the most liberating feeling a person can experience. I've lived under my freedom, and I've lived under God's freedom, and there is no comparison.

My freedom could have cost me my life. It probably should have. I very easily could have been one of those wrestlers who overdosed in a lonely hotel room.

I never appreciated life until I accepted Jesus Christ as my Savior. Until then, I never understood the paradox that the key to living a life of freedom is to give up freedom.

There is freedom, I learned, in not thinking I can go out and do anything I want. I've given up some of my rights. It requires humility to serve a holy God. It takes choosing to obey without feeling like you're a child.

The reward is *freedom*—freedom from the guilt and shame of knowing you weren't the best you could be. It's liberating to comprehend that nothing can separate me from the love of God. That's not a get-out-of-jail-free card, but the forgiveness that God gives — one rooted in mercy and grace — makes you aware that you can't keep doing what you did before. Actually, God's forgiveness transforms you so that you *don't* keep doing what you did before.

It's an amazing feeling to know that the Creator of the universe is pleased with you.

I know how happy it makes my kids to know that their dad is pleased with them. Who doesn't want that feeling? I have that same feeling, but with greater magnitude, with my heavenly Father.

If I could pick one group of people I would most like to talk to, it would be those who struggle in living the Christian life. Hey, eternity is going to be great! I look forward to it every day. But Christians face problems every day in the here and now. We do go through difficult times. We do get hurt.

Sometimes, to help us grow in our faith, God chooses to be silent for a short time. I know, it may not seem like a short time, but in the big picture, it really is. Yet, because God seems to be silent doesn't mean He isn't there. He is with us every step of the way, drawing us closer in relationship to Him because He knows that the absolute best thing for us is to put our trust completely in Him. Not partially, but completely. If it takes getting a scar for us to understand what God intends for us, so be it.

It pains me to think about kids who get beaten down on a daily basis, as by school classmates, for being a Christian. Peer pressure is vicious. It's cruel. The battering can be nonstop. I've been there, too, as a public personality and made it through by relying on knowing who I am in Christ and who He has made me to be. I've learned to place more value in what God thinks of me than what other people think of me.

Being a Christian can be difficult. That's not a theory or something I've read about. I know that from personal experience. But I also can offer this encouragement: No matter what we go through, there is something good on the other side to look forward to.

When I wrestled, I didn't like to train and diet. If another wrestler asked if I wanted to go to the gym with him, I needed to know how long we would be there. I needed to know the end was in sight.

I loved my chocolate chip cookies too. That's one reason my family always celebrated the completion of *WrestleManias* with pizza and cookies. I had to diet and work out so I would be in good shape and put on a good show. But in the gym I pictured the tasty batch of chocolate chip cookies on the other side of *WrestleMania*.

I'm an athlete. I'm goal-oriented. I need to have a purpose, even for working out and dieting.

After I got saved, I discovered Christians have a beautiful word for that on-the-other-side mentality: hope.

Tests, trials, and tribulations are only for a season. They never have the final say. Even death doesn't have the final say. I don't fear dying. I don't mean that I want to die. I don't want to leave this earth, because I love being with my wife, I enjoy being a part of my children's lives and watching them grow up. But I know where I am headed after I die. I know where I will be for eternity.

When I returned to wrestling, I went back a changed man, able to tell stories at deeper levels than I had before because I had adopted a new way of thinking. I went back into a world where thinking about Jesus was way down toward the bottom of the list of priorities.

I never walked through that curtain on the path to the ring without first getting on my knees and praying to ask God what He wanted me to do to glorify Him. I also would kneel and pray out in the arena or stadium as a way of shining my light in the darkness. I was asked many times what I prayed. I didn't have a standard prayer, but often it was something along the lines of "Lord, help me." That simple. All I wanted was for God to help me be a good witness on the platform He had brought me back to.

Then after the match, it was back through that curtain and into the locker room. Where before, cocky and out of control, I would challenge the other wrestlers to "Follow that!" I now returned in a different way. There were no arrogant declarations or challenges. Instead,

I wanted the others, some of whom doubted my salvation was for real, to see a humbled man whose changed life boldly declared, "Follow Christ!"

To me, wrestling can appear so silly in comparison to what is most important in life. Yet God took this wretch of a guy, still gifted at my job but beaten up physically, forgave me of my sins, brought me back to wrestling, and lifted me higher than I thought possible.

All glory is God's.

ACKNOWLEDGMENTS

I have to give many thanks, so bear with me. My family—Rebecca, Cameron, and Cheyenne—who continue to support and stick by my side as we go through this journey together. My parents, brothers, and sister, who have also supported me in all I do. My WWE family, who never gave up on me and welcomed me back.

Pastors John and Matthew Hagee and everyone associated with Cornerstone Church, who selflessly offered their help in all steps of my salvation and beyond. Keith and Priscilla Parker, whose love and discipleship were such a huge help to me.

Keith Mark and my *MacMillan River Adventures* family, the rose is off the bloom, the luster of doing an Outdoor show with the ex-WWE guy has worn off ... and y'all do it anyway! Thank you!

Chris Stuart (for making that phone call days after I retired from WWE) and everyone at Encore Sports and Entertainment for working so hard to get this book done.

Everyone at HarperCollins and Zondervan for taking the chance on the "Wrestling Guy" and allowing him to tell his story.

And David Thomas, who helped write this book. I appreciate your patience, dedication, and hard work in every step of the process.

Catch Shawn Michaels on the award-winning, Shawn Michaels "MacMillan River Adventures" show on the Outdoor Channel.

If you want to see episodes from previous seasons of MRA, visit www.mrahunting.com to find out how you can become an MRA VIP today and get caught up on the exciting adventures that you have missed!

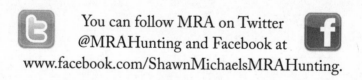

You can follow MRA on Twitter @MRAHunting and Facebook at www.facebook.com/ShawnMichaelsMRAHunting.

Find out more about what Shawn is up to currently
by following him on Twitter and Facebook:

Twitter: www.twitter.com/shawnmichaels

Facebook: www.facebook.com/theShawnMichaels

Shawn + Marty   Jose Lothario
Sensational Sherri
Kevin Nash
HHH

Kliq
Kevin Nash
Scot Hall
Kid (Sean Waltman)

D-Generation X   Marty - 127
  Shawn   HHH after Screw - 133
  Hunter   job in Shawn's room
  Cyna
  Rick Rude   Hunter Intros Shawn
                                H of F

                    God vs McMahons
                          98 1. Backlidon
                              2. Offensive

Mentors - 142
  Jose Morton
  Ricky Gibson
  Robert Gibson
  Terry Taylor

Mid South

Central State Wrestling Watt sent him to
KC 250-350
Southwest Champ Wrest. 500 (San Antonio)
AWA Wayne wants Team - Midnight Rockers
WWF
Birmingham
Memphis (AWA)
WWF

Single -
Sherri Martel
Kevin Nash - Diesel   93-95 2 Dudes w/
Hunter   attitude

Rebecca - 136
Sent tapes 128

HHH
Kevin Nash
Bret Hart
Rebecca - wife
Cameron 2000
Keith Parker - pastor + wife Dricella 145
Bruce Prichard - p.49
Keith Mark - TV cohost 67
Joe Lothario first coach: Dead
Rock + Roll Express 79
Daniel Bryan - trained him
Tony Falk III
Cheyenne - daughter
Cameron - son
Ric Flair
Pastor Hagee 148

Mark
@ 250, 300
in K.C.
128

Bible study
Group
149

to be read?
Line about doing drugs
Pg 55

Didn't like myself
Pg 55

Tyson 26
Stone cold

Legacy doesn't matter
77

Parkers 145